Parliament in the 1980s

To our respective parents

Parliament in the 1980s

Edited by Philip Norton

Basil Blackwell

© Basil Blackwell Ltd 1985

First published 1985

Basil Blackwell Ltd
108 Cowley Road, Oxford OX4 1JF, UK

Basil Blackwell Inc.
432 Park Avenue South, Suite 1505,
New York, NY 10016, USA

British Library Cataloguing in Publication Data

Parliament in the 1980s.
  1. Great Britain. *Parliament*
  I. Norton, Philip
  328.41   JN549
  ISBN 0–631–14056–5
  ISBN 0–631–14057–3 Pbk

Library of Congress Cataloging in Publication Data

Main entry under title:
Parliament in the 1980s.
  Bibliography: p.
  Includes index.
  1. Great Britain. Parliament–Addresses, essays, lectures, 2. Great Britain–
Politics and government–1979- –Addresses, essays, lectures, I. Norton, Philip.
JN549.P36 1985   328.41   85–1299
ISBN 0–631–14056–5
ISBN 0–631–14057–3 (pbk.)

Typeset by Oxford Publishing Services
Printed in Great Britain by Billing & Sons Ltd, Worcester

Contents

Preface

Parliament, especially the House of Commons, has been the subject of a number of textbooks and academic analyses. However, for any student of Parliament, one problem remains: it is difficult to keep abreast of changes in the institution. Despite what some critics may say, Parliament is not a static body. Recent years in particular have witnessed major developments in both Houses. This work has a simple aim: it seeks to identify and to analyse those developments. It is written for the sixth-form and undergraduate student of British politics, keen to gain an up-to-date supplement to existing but dated texts.

The book pursues a specific theme: the contribution of recent changes – behavioural, structural and representational – to the better fulfilment of Parliament's function of 'scrutiny and influence'. As far as possible, though, each chapter has been written as a self-contained whole. The work can thus be read in whole or in part, adaptable to different course structures.

As editor, my thanks are owing to my fellow contributors, all of whom have responded willingly to editorial requests and recommendations. All are graduates of Hull University and former students of mine, chosen because of the research they have carried out recently in the areas covered by the book. For reading and commenting upon portions of the manuscript, I am especially grateful to Michael Wheeler-Booth, David Beamish and Ken Batty. My intellectual debts, and those of my fellow contributors, will be apparent from the notes.

The book aims to fill a gap in the current literature on Parliament. Whether it succeeds in that aim is for the reader to determine. In any event, I welcome comments from interested readers.

Philip Norton
Department of Politics
University of Hull

I

Introduction
Parliament in Perspective

Philip Norton

In seeking to identify and analyse the role of Parliament in the British political system, two approaches can be employed: the historical and the comparative. The historical considers the development of Parliament over a period of time and is the approach most commonly employed by British writers. It constitutes, in effect, looking at Parliament on a vertical plane. The comparative approach entails looking at Parliament in relation to other legislatures. This horizontal approach is less often employed, certainly by British students of Parliament. Most useful is a combination of the two. Looking at Parliament from both a historical and a comparative perspective, two generalizations are possible:

(1) Parliaments, as formal institutions, are firmly entrenched in advanced and many less advanced industrialized nations. Both western liberal and communist regimes feel the need to have some form of national assembly or parliament with responsibility for giving formal assent to measures of public policy. The British Parliament may enjoy a greater longevity than most other (but not all) national assemblies, but it is merely one among a great many. Regardless of their impact on public policy, such assemblies continue to exist so long as there remains mass and elite acceptance of their legitimacy as agents of assent. In the British context, this means that Parliament will continue to exist as an entrenched and central institution of the formal political system. The existence of Parliament, as a parliament, is not under serious challenge.
(2) The functions ascribed to parliaments – the role they play in their respective political systems – are not static. The form of

parliaments may remain, but what is expected of them will change as political conditions change. Parliaments do not operate in a political vacuum. (If they were to, they would run the risk of ceasing to exist.) They are, as various authorities have noted, politically adaptable institutions. Hence, as Kenneth Wheare once observed, the variety of names accorded them: parliaments, legislatures, congresses and so on. Over time, the functions ascribed to a parliament or national assembly may be added to, modified or dispensed with. Parliaments often have to fulfil quite different functions (other than that of assent) within their respective political systems. Nonetheless, despite a variation in functions, a secular trend can be discerned. The nineteenth century has been viewed as the heyday of parliamentarianism, a time when parliaments occupied central roles in the making of public policy. Since then, the pressures of democracy and industrialization have led to a 'decline' in parliamentarianism, political systems having become more dominated by the executive. Parliaments have become less central – indeed, in some analyses, have become peripheral – to the setting of the political agenda and the resolution of issues on that agenda. Functions previously ascribed to them have been modified or dispensed with. Some remain more powerful than others (the US Congress usually being put forward as an example of the most powerful such body) but the historical trend has been clear.

For the student of parliament, the problem is one of discerning trends that are common to parliaments – the decline in parliamentarianism – and those that are specific to one particular parliament. The distinction is a central one in the study of the British Parliament. The secular trend identified above applies well to it. It enjoyed what some observers have described as a 'Golden Age' in the nineteenth century. That Golden Age was to die under pressures that were not unique to Britain, though they were to be exacerbated by political and constitutional features that characterized the British polity. A consequence of these pressures was that Parliament lost certain of the functions ascribed to it. Its capacity to fulfil the functions remaining to it was circumscribed by the twentieth-century growth of the welfare state and the managed economy. In more recent years, its capacity to fulfil certain of its functions has been limited by disparate developments external to it, developments which (when expressed in general terms) are not peculiar to Britain. In short, Parliament has been subject to the pressures that have been responsible for a decline in parliamentarianism. However, in recent years, there have been developments *internal* to Parliament, developments which have strengthened the ability of both Houses to fulfil certain of the functions ascribed to them and developments which, in combination, are peculiar to Parliament in Britain. The purpose of this work is primarily to identify those internal developments and to analyse their effects. Let us first of all, though, consider the wider external developments and their effect upon Parliament in the twentieth century.

'Decline' and Functions

For a brief period in the nineteenth century, Parliament played a role as a partner in government. Pressure for franchise reform, not least from non-landed industrialists and entrepreneurs, generated an extension of the franchise. The change, embodied in the Reform Act of 1832, was a modest one. The extent of the change was sufficient to loosen the grip of the aristocracy and of the ministry on the House of Commons (seats were less easy to purchase) but not so extensive as to require the creation of organized and mass-membership political parties. Members achieved a degree of independence in their parliamentary behaviour, producing a House of Commons that was willing to reject and to modify measures and, indeed, to participate in the shaping of measures. With the exception of the period from 1841 to 1846, party cohesion was almost unknown. This was the period referred to as the Golden Age of Parliament. It proved to be short-lived.

Pressure for further extension of the franchise, political expediency and some measure of paternalism resulted in the passage in 1867 of the Second Reform Act. With subsequent Acts, this served to extend the franchise beyond the middle class. With the passage of the 1884 Representation of the People Act, a majority of working men were given the vote. Electors were now too numerous to be bribed, at least by individual candidates. Contact and persuasion were possible on an extended scale only through the use of extensive and well-organized parties. As a result, both main parties developed from cadre into mass-membership organizations geared to reaching the new voters. Party organization came to dominate political life. The effect on Parliament was two-fold.

First, within Parliament, the dominance of the House of Commons over the Upper House was assured. As traditional authority gave way to and was superseded by notions of rational-legal authority, so the

House of Lords could not maintain its claim to be coequal with the elected Lower House. This change in relationship was to be well recognized in the later decades of the century, though not until 1911 was the Lords forced into formal acceptance – with the passage of the Parliament Act – of its diminished status.

Second, within the political system, functions previously ascribed to Parliament were effectively transferred elsewhere. The elective function – that of choosing the government – was passed downward to the electorate. The legislative function – more generally the making of public policy – was passed upward to the Cabinet. By the end of the century, Parliament played a secondary role in the determination of public policy. Members of Parliament were dependent upon their party label for election and upon their party leaders for promotion. The electoral fortunes of MPs depended primarily upon the success or failure of the government. Failure of government backbenchers to vote for their own side could result not only in the loss of a measure but also, on votes of confidence, in a dissolution. It was a prospect relished neither by backbenchers nor by their constituency parties. Party loyalty, institutional pressures and personal ambition thus combined to propel MPs into following the party line. The consequence, given (usually but not always) a basic two-party system, was that government could rely upon, indeed take for granted, a parliamentary majority for its measures. Policy-making became pre-eminently a function of government.

After these developments, what functions remained that Parliament was expected to fulfil? None are prescribed in any one formally binding or authoritative document. Some observers identify a variety of functions, others list only two or three.[1] An analysis of writings on Parliament, of constitutional practice and of parliamentary behaviour would suggest three primary ones: those of providing the personnel of government, of legitimization, and of subjecting measures of public policy to scrutiny and influence. This is to identify them in rather bald terms. Each is in need of qualification and amplification.

Providing the personnel of government

This is the least problematic of the functions. By convention, ministers are drawn from and remain within Parliament. Again by convention, most ministers – including the Prime Minister and most members of the Cabinet — are drawn from the elected chamber. (No less than two but rarely more than four peers are appointed now to the Cabinet.) There is no formal prohibition on a Prime Minister appointing as a minister someone who is neither an MP or a peer; such occasions are rare but not unknown.[2] However, those given office are normally then elevated to the peerage or (more riskily) seek a Commons seat through the medium of a by-election. In practice, most ministers have served a parliamentary apprenticeship of several years before their appointments. Parliament provides both the personnel of government and the forum in which those seeking office can make their mark. Though there are occasional calls for non-parliamentarians (businessmen, industrialists and the like) to be brought into government, this function of Parliament arouses no serious debate or controversy.

Legitimization

Most national assemblies exist for the purpose of giving assent to measures of public policy. Indeed, this constitutes the primary purpose for which representatives of the local English communities (*communes*) were first summoned in the thirteenth century. Today, the broad rubric of legitimization encompasses different elements. The most obvious and the most significant is that of manifest legitimization. This constitutes the formal giving of assent to measures, enabling them to be designated Acts of Parliament; such Acts are accepted as having general and binding applicability by virtue of having been passed by the country's elected or part-elected national assembly (the elected chamber now having dominance within that assembly). A second element is that of latent legitimization. The government derives its primary political legitimacy from being elected through (if no longer by) the House of Commons. The collectivity of ministers that form the government enjoy enhanced legitimacy also by being drawn from and remaining in Parliament. For Parliament as an institution, this of course constitutes an essentially passive function.

There are two other sub-functions that fall under the heading of legitimization: those of tension-release and support-mobilization. By meeting and debating issues, Parliament provides an outlet, an authoritative outlet, for the expression of different views within society. Thus it plays an important part in the dissipation of tension. For example, during the Falklands crisis in 1982, Parliament provided the authoritative forum for the expression of public feelings on the issue. In Argentina, by contrast, citizens enjoyed no such body through which their views could be expressed and were forced instead to take to the streets to make their feelings known. Parliament also seeks to mobilize public support for measures which it has approved. In essence, these two sub-functions constitute a two-way process between electors and the elected, the views of citizens being channelled through Parliament (tension-release) and Parliament then mobilizing support for those measures which it has approved (support-mobilization). In practice, the extent to which Parliament is capable of fulfilling these functions has been much overlooked and, when considered by writers, has often been found wanting.

Scrutiny and influence

Parliament ceased to be a policy-making legislature in the nineteenth century. Instead it acquired the characteristics of what I have elsewhere termed a policy-influencing legislature.[3] It ceased to be involved in the making of public policy, but it was expected to subject such policy to a process of scrutiny and influence. Scrutiny and influence are analytically separable terms, but scrutiny without any consequent sanction to effect influence is of little worth; and influence is best and most confidently attempted when derived from prior scrutiny. Hence, scrutiny and influence may be conjoined as a single function of Parliament. It is, in practice, its most debated and contentious function.

The exercise of scrutiny and influence can be seen to operate at two levels. These, in simple terms, may be characterized as being at the macro and the micro level of public policy. At the macro level, Parliament is expected to subject measures of public policy, embodied in legislative bills or in executive actions, to scrutiny and influence prior to giving assent to them. It is essentially a reactive function, exercised at a moderately late stage in the policy cycle: this is illustrated in figure 1.1. It is one which is most often carried out through the party elements in both Houses, the official Opposition or, nowadays, opposition parties seeking to exert the most sustained scrutiny of government measures. However, Parliament is but one of many influences at work in the policy cycle and, by virtue of what is usually an assured government majority at the end of the scrutinizing process, is rarely deemed to be the most important. Indeed, in some analyses, it is of no great importance at all.

At the micro level, Parliament is expected to scrutinize and respond to the effects of policy on the community. In practice, this task is exercised less through the party elements and Parliament as a collective entity, and more through Members of Parliament as Constituency representatives. Members represent territorially designated areas (constituencies) and seek to defend and pursue the interests of their constituents and groups within their constituencies. Whereas

STAGES OF POLICY DEVELOPMENT	ACTORS			FACTORS LIMITING PARLIAMENTARY IMPACT
	Primary	Proximate	Marginal	
GESTATION Genesis	Party Interest groups		Select committees Party committees in Commons	Party-dominated, two-party system; centralized; government dependence on diverse groups.
Access to government	Ministers → Senior civil servants		Parliamentary Party	
PROPOSAL PREPARATION Formulation	Cabinet committees Cabinet Senior civil servants			'Closed' government centralized; hierarchical; complexity of legislation.
Acceptance by government	Cabinet Cabinet committees Ministers	Interest groups Parliamentary Party		
Formal construction	Parliamentary Counsel	House of Commons		
Committal to next stage	Cabinet legislation committee →	House of Commons	(House of Lords)	
DELIBERATION AND ADOPTION ↳ Scrutiny	→ House of Commons—(House of Lords) (also groups *de facto*?)	Party Interest groups Constituents		*Ad hoc* committees; dependence on government; party majority; hierarchical.
Legitimation and adoption	→ House of Commons—(House of Lords)			
IMPLEMENTATION Carrying out of policy	Affected bodies Govt agencies Officials		House of Commons	Absence (pre-1979) of comprehensive, permanent investigative committees.
Policy evaluation and response	Affected groups Agencies Departments	Select committees Party committees in Commons		

Figure 1.1 Policy development process in Britain

Source: P. Norton, 'Parliament and Policy in Britain: The House of Commons as a Policy Influencer', *Teaching Politics*, 13(2), 1984, p. 207.

at the macro level MPs will be concerned to debate the principle of public policy, usually within the context of party ideology, at the micro level they are much more concerned with the policy's practical implications for their constituents.

In terms of the working life of Parliament, scrutiny and influence constitute its most demanding function. Seeking to subject government actions and legislative measures to scrutiny and a degree of influence occupies most of Parliament's time and energies. It is also the function that attracts the most debate and criticism. At best, effective fulfilment of the function allows Parliament to set the broad limits within which government can govern. (At the end of the day, it retains the formal sanction to deny assent to the government's legislative proposals and its request for supply.) At worst, the function may be fulfilled in the most superficial of ways, providing no effective check upon the executive. According to critics, it is the latter description which has accorded more closely to reality over past decades.

Certainly, Parliament's ability to fulfil this function has been affected adversely by the growth of government responsibilities in the twentieth century. The growth of the welfare state and the managed economy generated not only larger government departments and greatly increased expenditure but also a mass of legislation, difficult for Parliament to deal with because of its extent and, more significantly perhaps, because of its complexity. Parliament itself failed to generate an institutional capacity to keep abreast of these developments. As government intervention in the economic and social life of the nation expanded, so ministers became more dependent upon diverse groups operating in these sectors. Policy increasingly was made by government in conjunction with outside groups; the locus of policy-making moved even further from Parliament. And when policy was presented eventually to Parliament for deliberation, the two Houses lacked an effective means of subjecting it to sustained and informed scrutiny.

A growing awareness of these deficiencies generated calls for parliamentary reform. The reforms advocated were varied, and in the case of the House of Lords were as much directed to the question of composition as to that of functions. Reformers, though, were generally united in the end result which they sought: a Parliament capable of subjecting government to an effective process of scrutiny and influence, of providing generally the broad limits within which government could govern. Calls for reform gained momentum in the 1960s and 1970s as Parliament appeared to be buffeted by developments that undermined or limited it ability to fulfil the functions ascribed to it. What, then, were these developments? And what has been Parliament's response?

External Challenges

Disparate developments, external to Parliament, have served to challenge or to undermine its functions of legitimization and of scrutiny and influence. The legitimacy of Parliament to fulfil the central function of giving assent to measures of public policy has been challenged by the use of referendums, by the unwillingness of some groups to accept the hegemony of Parliament's authority, and by the continuing debate on the 'representativeness' of Parliament – whether the concern is with the electoral system, developments within the Labour Party, or the hereditary basis of the House of Lords. (The greater polarization of debate within the House of Commons may also have served to exacerbate its difficulties in fulfilling the role of support-mobilization.) The capacity of both Houses to carry out the function of scrutiny and influence has been greatly limited by the locus of policy-making moving further away from Westminster – a consequence of British membership of the European Communities, of tripartism and of sectorization in domestic policy-making. The problem is aggravated by the continuing and deeply embedded secretiveness of British government and, from June 1983 onwards, by an overwhelming government majority in the House of Commons.

The 1970s witnessed referendums on membership of the European Communities (UK-wide), on the government's devolution proposals (in Scotland and Wales), and, in Northern Ireland, on the issue of the border. The implications of their use, as John Mackintosh observed, 'was that majorities in the House of Commons did not confer sufficient authority or legitimacy to a decision when this was of the utmost importance'.[4] No clear line was or has been drawn between those issues which were and those which were not amenable to resolution by referendum. There have been calls for referendums on capital punishment, on electoral reform (a call currently made by Vernon Bogdanor), and on trade-union reform, a possibility raised by Mrs Thatcher when Leader of the Opposition. In short, there now exists the opportunity for disparate groups to press the case for 'their' cause to be submitted to the people for determination, instead of leaving it to be decided by Parliament. In other words, the decisions of Parliament may cease to be seen by many groups as definitive.

A number of groups have also displayed an unwillingness to accept the decisions of Parliament as binding upon their members, not because those decisions have not been submitted to the people for their approval but because they have not received the prior assent of their members. That this should be so is explicable given the economic downturn of the 1960s and 1970s. As governments moved to pursue redistributive instead of distributive economic policies (the economic cake having ceased to expand), groups affected adversely by government policies became less willing to accept those policies, even where given the formal assent of Parliament. Among those giving voice to the unwillingness to accept Parliament's decisions as binding upon their members have been a number of trade-union leaders. As Gillian Peele observed, the trade unions denied or appeared to deny the legitimacy of the 1971 Industrial Relations Act 'and it often seemed that the unions denied also the general right of Parliament to pass legislation to regulate industrial relations.'[5] In recent years, trade-union leaders such as Arthur Scargill have given the impression that they wish to reserve to the unions an exclusive decisional and legitimizing function in the sphere of industrial relations.

The legitimacy of Parliament to fulfil the definitive function of giving assent on behalf of the electorate has also been called in question by challenges to the representative basis of both Houses. The growth of third-party challenges to the existing two-party dominance in the 1970s and early 1980s – especially the creation of the Social Democratic Party (in 1981) and the SDP/Liberal Alliance in the 1983 general election – served to emphasize the disparity between votes received (nationally) and parliamentary seats won under the first-past-the-post plurality method of election. Advocates of electoral reform stress the unrepresentative, or non-proportional, nature of the electoral system on which the House of Commons is returned.[6] The representative nature of the House is questioned also by developments within the Labour Party. The concept of intra-party democracy, a central tenet of Labour Party organization, has underpinned pressure from within the party for Labour MPs to be more responsive to the wishes and dictates of their local parties. In 1980, the Labour Party Conference confirmed an earlier decision that sitting Labour Members be subject to a compulsory reselection procedure. Critics contended that the effect was to shift even further Members' responsiveness from the totality of constituents to local party activists. Questioning of the representative nature of the House of Commons has served also to underline the unrepresentative nature of the Upper House. Peers represent no one but themselves (their writs of summons are personal). Their Lordships' House has been vulnerable to calls for reform for over a century. Following the failure of the 1969 Parliament (No. 2) Bill, pressure for more radical reform built up within the Labour Party. In 1977 the Labour Party Conference approved a motion calling for 'an efficient single-chamber legislating body', reaffirming its commitment in 1980.

Parliament has not been in a position satisfactorily to fulfil the task of support-mobilization. Government secrecy and government control over parliamentary procedures have left Parliament with little independent scope – or knowledge – to carry out that task. In many respects, the greater polarization of parliamentary parties could be seen as having weakened it, further detracting from the capacity of the institution to act as a collective entity.

The ability of Parliament to subject government to effective scrutiny and influence is challenged by the movement of the locus of policy-making further from government – which has a direct relationship with Parliament – to bodies which have no such direct relationship. The locus of policy-making in various sectors has moved upwards, to a supra-national body (the European Communities), and downwards, to disparate 'policy communities'.

The United Kingdom became a member of the European Communities on 1 January 1973. Under the provisions of the 1972 European Communities Act, all existing as well as future EC legislation was to have general and binding applicability in the United Kingdom. Such legislation was promulgated by bodies to which the UK was able to make only a limited, or minority, contribution and with which (after the introduction of direct elections to the European Parliament in 1979) the UK Parliament as such had no direct or formal relationship. Given the provisions of the 1972 Act, Parliament was not called upon to give its assent to EC legislation. Subjecting such legislation, or draft legislation, to scrutiny generated significant problems for an institution not geared to membership of a supra-national body.

As its responsibilities have grown, government has become more dependent upon interest groups, not only for advice and data but also for co-operation in the implementation of policy. In the 1960s and 1970s, with a relative decline in resources, government encountered greater difficulty in achieving the support or acquiescence of the different groups affected by proposed or actual policies. At one level, the attempt by government to gain the support of 'peak' organizations took the form of tripartism. Economic policy was often discussed in conjunction with representatives of the Trades Union Congress and the Confederation of British Industry. The most notable impact of the influence of such organizations was manifested in 1976 when the Chancellor of the Exchequer made a 3 per cent reduction in income tax conditional on the acceptance by trade unions of pay restraint. The TUC was being invited to exercise a power that was vested formally in Parliament. In practice, such government/'peak'-organization contact has tended to be bipartite rather than tripartite and has been less apparent since the return of a Conservative government in 1979. More continuous and pervasive has been the 'sectorization' of policy-making, policy emerging from negotiations in disparate policy communities between civil servants and representatives of groups within that community.[7] The policy agreed upon is then 'sold' to the rest of government, percolating up for Cabinet approval (if the policy is important enough to require it) and then for parliamentary assent. Most day-to-day, or incremental, policy is generated through this process, a process having no direct linkage with Parliament and one which produces policy changes that may not have to be submitted to Parliament for assent. Even where such submission is necessary, Parliament may have neither the knowledge nor the time to subject the changes to sustained or competent scrutiny.

These changes are clearly significant, having wide and major implications for the British polity as a whole and not just for Parliament. The importance of some should not be exaggerated: referendums, for example, appear to have less appeal now than in the 1970s; tripartism is out of fashion. The effect of some of the others, such as membership of the European Communities, is difficult to over-emphasize. In combination, they pose a significant challenge to Parliament's ability to fulfil the functions remaining to it.

Has Parliament managed to reform itself in a way that allows it to respond to these disparate external challenges? The answer is yes, partially. The way in which and the extent to which it has responded are considered in parts I and II of this book. The direction in which, in the eyes of critics, it still has to go in order to achieve a more effective response will be discussed in the conclusion.

Internal Reinforcements

Over the past decade or so, Parliament has experienced significant reforms and changes in behaviour. Some of these constitute a conscious attempt to establish more effective scrutiny of the executive. Others are the product of unrelated causes which, in combination, are unique to Parliament in Britain. Both the House of Commons and the House of Lords have witnessed (different) behavioural and structural changes; in both Houses, the former have facilitated the latter. The House of Commons has also witnessed, over a longer period of time, changes in MP–constituency relationships, changes not possible in the unelected House of Lords. These various changes are explored in detail in the succeeding chapters. As a prelude to what follows, they need only a brief delineation here.

Behavioural changes

In the 1970s, and continuing into the 1980s, both Houses witnessed significant changes in behaviour and attitude. In the Commons, the behavioural changes preceded and were then reinforced by a change in attitudes. In the Lords, an attitudinal change appeared to act as a spur to changes in behaviour.

In the Upper House, the behavioural changes encompassed sitting more often and for longer hours. However, in both Houses the most significant change was in voting behaviour. MPs and peers ceased to vote predictably. In the 1970–4 Parliament, with a Conservative majority of over 30 in the House of Commons and an in-built Conservative majority in the House of Lords, the Heath government could have been expected to take for granted a majority in both Houses for the measures it presented. In the event, in the Lower House it witnessed extensive and persistent cross-voting by dissident backbenchers. It was defeated in the division lobbies on six occasions, three of the defeats taking place on three-line whips. In the Upper House it was defeated 25 times. Since then, neither House has looked back. In the 14 years since the 1970 general election, the number of government defeats in Parliament (Commons and Lords) has exceeded 500 (table 1.1). This, not surprisingly, is without precedent in the twentieth-century history of Parliament.

These behavioural changes are identified and analysed in chapters 2 and 5. Given the incidence of government defeats, the change in behaviour by MPs and peers has clearly had some impact upon public policy, in a number of cases very significantly so. What, then, explains this change in behaviour? In chapter 2, I argue that in the Commons it was Edward Heath's prime ministerial leadership which acted as the crucial spur in ensuring that dissenting Conservative backbenchers expressed their dissent in the public form of cross-voting in the division lobbies. One consequence was the six defeats already referred to, creating a precedent for succeeding Parliaments. Combined with

Table 1.1   Government defeats in Parliament from 1970 to summer recess 1984

| Parliament | Number of defeats | |
	House of Commons	House of Lords
1970–4	6	25
1974	17	15
1974–9	42	347
1979–83	1	45
1983–4	1[a]	19

[a]The vote went against government advice, though it was not a formally whipped vote.

the effects of the 1974 general elections (minority government followed by government with a minute overall majority), this created the conditions that allowed for an unprecedented number of government defeats in the period from 1974 to 1979. The more defeats there were, the more MPs began to appreciate the effect that cross-voting could have: towards the end of the decade, there was a perceptible shift in many Members' attitudes from deferential to participant. This change in attitude was carried on in to succeeding Parliaments, resulting in government backbenchers being prepared on occasion to threaten the government's majority.

This combination of factors (Edward Heath's leadership, the results of the two 1974 elections) was unique to the British House of Commons. The changes in the Upper House, not surprisingly (given the uniqueness of the institution) were also peculiar to that body. As identified by Nicholas Baldwin in chapter 5, the two primary factors underpinning their Lordships' change in behaviour were (a) the effect of the influx of life peers (more active, more crossbenchers) and (b) a realization that reform of the Upper House was unlikely to take place. Given this latter perception – and a growing feeling, especially after the 1983 general election, that the Commons' ability to scrutinize government effectively was in some doubt – the members of the Upper House decided that it was up to them to make their House work. This resulted in the House sitting more often, for longer hours, with more peers present, and with their Lordships prepared to be even more independent than hitherto in their voting behaviour, especially under a Conservative government. In the words of one official of the Lords, the House was no longer the Gentleman's Club it had been when he first started working there.[8] Their Lordships were now prepared to use their existing powers with a greater degree of confidence than before.

This greater independence on the part of MPs and peers not only ensured that they were able to exert a greater degree of scrutiny and influence on the floor of their respective chambers, it also encouraged the creation of bodies capable of exercising the task of scrutiny on a more regular and sustained basis than was possible on the floor of either House. The behavioural changes in both Houses underpinned the structural changes.

Structural changes

Prior to the 1970s, committees of investigation (select committees) were not prominent features of the parliamentary landscape. Indeed, in the sphere of public policy and legislation, they were a remarkable rarity in the Upper House. In the Lower House, the committee stage of legislation was normally taken in standing committee, but select committees were not much in evidence. The latter half of the 1960s witnessed the 'Crossman reforms', including the modest experiment with select committees on science and technology and on agriculture. It was not until the 1970s, however, that such committees emerged to become significant in terms of parliamentary activity and as agents for fulfilling the task of scrutiny and influence.

The extent and effect of the greater use of committees is explored in chapters 3 and 6. In 1979, the House of Commons acquired for the first time in its history a comprehensive or near-comprehensive set of select committees to scrutinize the work of government departments. Though limited by the absence of formal sanctions, by limited resources, by competing demands on Members' time, and by some confusion as to their precise role, the committees constitute a marked improvement on what preceded them. They enjoy control of their own schedules and topics for enquiry, they have acquired by dint of experience some effective interviewing capacity, and enjoy some political attention. They have effected a number of shifts in government policy that without their existence would presumably not have taken place. They are the most prominent of a number of structural and procedural reforms implemented in the Commons in recent years. These other reforms are listed in appendix 1. Like the select committees, most owe their existence and their sustenance to the attitudinal change which has taken place in the Commons; they were established at the behest not of government but of backbenchers.

Similar observations are possible about the structural changes in the Lords. Most prominent among the changes has been the creation and operation of the European Communities Committee. Working through seven sub-committees, it calls upon the services of nearly 100 peers. It has achieved a formidable reputation as an effective scrutineer of draft EC legislation and clearly overshadows its Commons counterpart. Membership of the European Communities provided the impetus for its creation, but that alone does not explain the extent and effect of its activity. For that, as Cliff Grantham and Caroline Moore Hodgson show in chapter 6, one has to look to the changes identified by Baldwin: the influx of active life peers and a willingness to make the institution work. Further, as they show, the committee's work has been facilitated by the absence of a party majority and by a general acceptance of British membership of the European Communities. Nor is the committee the Lord's only venture into the sphere of select committees. It has established a Committee on Science and Technology and in the last Parliament, a committee to consider the problem of unemployment. The government chief whip in the Lords, Lord Denham, has expressed the view – quoted in chapter 6 – that the EC Committee could prove to be the forerunner of a series of committees, covering domestic matters. In short, the reforms of the 1970s may encourage even more wide-ranging changes in the 1980s. For the House of Lords, the contrast with the 1950s and 1960s would be profound.

Representational changes

The behavioural and structural changes of the past 15 years have enabled both Houses to fulfil somewhat more effectively the function of scrutiny at the macro level of policy. Over a longer period of time, the House of Commons has witnessed a significant change in scrutiny at the micro level. Members of Parliament have been called upon to undertake a far greater amount of constituency casework and have done so, despite limited resources, with some success.

These 'representational' changes are analysed in chapter 4 by James Marsh. As government responsibilities have grown, the greater has been the number of complaints by individuals against agencies of government. As the resources available to government to meet group demands have declined, the greater has been the number of demands and complaints made by individual groups. There has in consequence been a significant increase in the demands made of MPs to represent to government the interests and demands of constituents and of groups within constituencies. Members have responded by devoting more time and resources to this aspect of their work. In the constituencies, this has entailed the regular holding of 'surgeries', the maintaining of an office and secretarial support; in some cases, it now extends to utilizing computers and word-processors. In Westminster, it has involved not only a greater use of Question Time but also, more extensively and effectively, correspondence with ministers. Each month, about 10,000 letters are written by MPs to ministers; ministers in the Department of Health and Social Security receive about 2,000 of these. In most cases, Members manage to achieve the response desired by their constituents. By acting as a channel (in constituents' eyes, the best-known channel) of communication between the citizen and government, Members fulfil an important tension-release function. It is a role with which constituents appear satisfied. A survey in 1978 found that of those who contacted their MP, 75 per cent reported a 'good' or 'very good' response.[9]

Individually, these various changes internal to Parliament may find a counterpart in other legislatures (new committee structures, more constituency casework), but collectively and in substance they are peculiar to Parliament in Britain. They have provided MPs and peers with a greater opportunity to fulfil in particular the function of scrutiny and influence, at both the macro and the micro levels of policy. The use of select committees has also provided the opportunity to fulfil a tension-release function, providing an authoritative forum (free of Government diktat) in which groups can make their views known; writing to the local MP can provide a similar service for the individual citizen. By being seen to fulfil these functions, Parliament may also serve to enhance its own legitimacy as a legitimizing body. Indeed, one of the most noteworthy influences of the House of Lords on outside opinion occurred in 1984. As a result of what the House did to the Local Government (Interim Provisions) Bill – the Bill paving the way for abolition of the Greater London Council – the left-wing leader of the GLC, Ken Livingstone, ceased to favour a unicameral legislature. Though by no means supporting the existing House, he accepted the need for a second chamber. On less committed individuals, the House may have had an even greater impact. Paradoxically, by being more assertive, the unelected House may have done more to ensure its own continuance than if it had done nothing.

Conclusion

For over a century, Parliament has not been a policy-making legislature. Instead, in common with most Commonwealth parliaments, it has been a policy-influencing legislature. Its functions within the political system have been limited, comprising those of legitimization (the essential function of most national assemblies), of providing the personnel of government, and of scrutiny and influence of legislation and executive actions. Its ability to fulfil those functions has been circumscribed by the growth of government in the twentieth century and by its failure to reform itself to keep abreast of that growth. In recent decades, external pressures have continued to limit or undermine its capacity to fulfil the functions ascribed to it. However, unlike in earlier decades (and unlike in other comparable legislatures), Parliament has experienced in recent years significant internal reforms – behavioural, structural and representational. These have contributed to the capacity of the institution to fulfil more effectively the function of scrutiny and influence. Hence, their implementation and their impact deserve attention. To ignore them would result in a distorted view of the contemporary British Parliament. Whether they need to be taken further – or whether more radical reforms are needed – will be considered in the conclusion. But any discussion of reform must be based on an awareness of what Parliament currently is and does and not just upon what it was and did in the decades of the 1950s and the 1960s.

Notes

1 The range of functions are considered in some detail in P. Norton, 'Parliament and Regime Support in Britain', paper presented to a conference on Parliaments and Regime Support, Duke University, USA, December 1982. This section draws upon that paper. See also P. Norton, *The Commons in Perspective* (Oxford: Martin Robertson, 1981), ch. 4.

2 The most recent example was in September 1984 when Mrs Thatcher appointed Mr David Young to the Cabinet as Minister without Portfolio. At the same time, the conferment of a peerage was announced.

3 P. Norton, 'Parliament and Policy in Britain: The House of Commons as a Policy Influencer', *Teaching Politics*, 13(2), May 1984, pp. 198–221.

4 J. Mackintosh (ed.), *People and Parliament* (Aldershot: Saxon House, 1978), p. 3.

5 G. Peele, 'The Developing Constitution', in C. Cook and J. Ramsden (eds), *Trends in British Politics since 1945* (London: Macmillan, 1978), p. 9.

6 See especially S. E. Finer (ed.), *Adversary Politics and Electoral Reform* (London: Wigram, 1975).

7 A. G. Jordan and J. J. Richardson, 'The British Policy Style or the Logic of Negotiation', in J. J. Richardson (ed.), *Policy Styles in Western Europe* (London: George Allen & Unwin, 1982), pp. 82–4.

8 One of the clerks of the House, addressing a group of teachers at the House of Lords, May 1984.
9 B. E. Cain, J. A. Ferejohn and M. P. Fiorina, 'The Roots of Legislator Popularity in Great Britain and the United States', *California Institute of Technology*: *Social Science Working Paper 288* (October 1979), pp. 6–7.

Part I

The House of Commons

2

Behavioural Changes
Backbench Independence in the 1980s

Philip Norton

Prior to 1970, various generalizations could be made about backbench behaviour in the House of Commons. The two most significant and observable concerning voting behaviour were: (a) MPs rarely if ever voted against their own side, and (b) on those rare occasions when government backbenchers did vote against their own side, they never did so in numbers sufficient to deny the government a majority. Cohesion was a much commented upon feature of parliamentary life. In his seminal work *Modern British Politics*, Samuel Beer referred to the 'Prussian discipline' of MPs. Day after day, he declared, MPs 'trooped into the division lobbies at the signals of their Whips and in the service of the authoritative decisions of their parliamentary parties.'[1] Party cohesion had increased 'until in recent decades it was so close to 100 per cent that there was no longer any point in measuring it'.[2] Such assertions were easily borne out by the empirical data. Indeed, so great was party cohesion on the Conservative side of the House that there were actually two sessions in the 1950s when not one Conservative MP cast a dissenting vote against the advice of the party whips. On those occasions in other sessions when some cross-voting did take place, it had no appreciable impact upon government. Not once between 1945 and 1970 was a government defeated because of its own supporters voting in the Opposition lobby. Throughout the post-war period up to 1970, Government appeared to have little to worry about in terms of dissent by its own backbenchers in the Commons' division lobbies. It could take its majority for granted.

So much for the period from 1945 to 1970. After 1970, backbench behaviour in the Commons' division lobbies changed dramatically. The generalizations descriptive of pre-1970 behaviour ceased to be applicable. Members of Parliament proved willing to vote against their own side and to do so on occasion with serious effect. So much so that by the early 1980s, Beer – who fifteen years earlier had been lamenting the regimented discipline of Members – was able to write in glowing terms of the rise of backbench independence. There was, he declared, an abrupt and radical discontinuity in the behaviour of MPs, dating from 1970 onwards.[3] Indeed, such were the changes taking place that Beer felt justified in referring to 'the rise of Parliament'.[4] According to another American observer, John Schwarz, the changes were such as to provide the House with a new role in policy-making.[5] Clearly, the House of Commons was a much changed body from that which had existed in earlier days.

To what extent, then, was there a change in backbench behaviour in the 1970s and to what extent has that change been continued in the 1980s? Just as importantly, what explains such a change, and what effect, if any, has it had? Has the House acquired a new role in policy-making or has the effect of greater backbench independence been a marginal one in terms of the activities of government? For some critics, the events of recent years have been of no great import. To some students of Parliament, they have been limited but significant, a useful guide to what the House of Commons could and should achieve in its relationship with that part of it which forms the government.

The Incidence of Backbench Dissent

That there was a change in backbench behaviour in the years after 1970 is easily demonstrated. However, that change has not been uniform. There are three distinct periods in the post–1970 era of backbench independence. The first is that of 1970 to 1979, encompassing three Parliaments (those of 1970–4, 1974 and 1974–9). The second is that of the Parliament of 1979 to 1983. The third is that of the present Parliament returned in June 1983. Though there is a linkage between the three periods, each has its own distinguishing characteristics.

The Parliaments of the 1970s

The three Parliaments of the 1970s were distinctive because of the extent to which MPs proved willing to vote against their own side in the Commons' division lobbies and to do so with serious effect. The increase in intra-party dissent in the division lobbies is demonstrated by the data in table 2.1. Whereas few divisions in the pre–1970

Table 2.1   Divisions witnessing dissenting votes, 1945–1979

Parliament (number of sessions in parenthesis)	Number of divisions witnessing dissenting votes			Number of divisions witnessing dissenting votes expressed as a percentage of all divisions
	Total	Lab.[a]	Con.[a]	
1945–50 (4)	87	79	27	7
1950–1 (2)	6	5	2	2.5
1951–5 (4)	25	17	11	3
1955–9 (4)	19	10	12	2
1959–64 (5)	137	26	120	13.5
1964–6 (2)	2	1	1	0.5
1966–70 (4)	124	109	41	9.5
1970–4 (4)	221	34[b]	204	20
1974 (1)	25	8	21	23
1974–9 (5)	423	309	240	28

[a]As one division may witness dissenting votes by Labour *and* Conservative Members, the Labour and Conservative figures do not necessarily add up to the totals on the left.
[b]Excluding the Labour backbench 'ginger group' votes of February–March 1971.

Source: P. Norton, *Dissension in the House of Commons 1974–1979* (Oxford: Oxford University Press, 1980), p. 248.

Parliaments had witnessed cross-voting, dissenting votes in the Parliaments of 1970 onwards were far from uncommon. In the Parliament of 1970–4, Conservative backbenchers proved willing to vote against their leaders not only on more occasions but in greater numbers than before. The same was true, only more so, of Labour backbenchers in the years from 1974 to 1979. The size of Labour dissenting lobbies in the post-war period is given in table 2.2. As it reveals, there were 44 divisions in the 1974–9 Parliament in which 50 or more Labour MPs voted against their own side. The incidence of cross-voting in the Parliament increased until, in the final session, almost one in two of every division witnessed dissenting votes cast by one or more Labour Members.[6] The 1970s, in short, witnessed an upsurge in cross-voting in the House of Commons' division lobbies. The change was of such a magnitude as to make invalid the generalization previously drawn as to the cohesion of MPs. The point was well summarized by Leon Epstein. 'It was clear', he observed,

that in the 1970s both Conservative and Labour MPs voted more independently, and more consequently so, than their predecessors of the 1950s. The

Table 2.2 Size of dissenting Labour lobbies, 1945–1979 (number of divisions in which Labour dissenters entered official Conservative lobby given in parenthesis)

Number of Labour dissenting voters	Number of divisions									
	1945–50	1950–1	1951–5	1955–9	1959–64	1964–6	1966–70	1970–4	1974	1974–9[a]
1 only	16 (14)	1 (0)	1 (1)	2 (0)	12 (7)	1 (1)	18 (13)	13 (7)	1 (1)	53 (32)
2–9	27 (15)	2 (1)	5 (0)	6 (1)	8 (0)	0 (0)	16 (4)	6 (2)	0 (0)	87 (41)
10–19	17 (4)	1 (0)	3 (0)	0 (0)	1 (0)	0 (0)	44 (1)[b]	5 (1)	1 (0)	49 (14)
20–9	5 (1)	0 (0)	2 (0)	0 (0)	4 (0)	0 (0)	10 (1)	1 (0)	1 (0)	31 (4)
30–9	9 (1)	1 (0)	2 (0)	1 (0)	0 (0)	0 (0)	10 (0)	3 (0)	2 (0)	20 (0)
40–9	4 (0)	0 (0)	1 (0)	0 (0)	1 (0)	0 (0)	5 (0)	3 (0)	2 (0)	25 (1)
50 or more	1 (0)	0 (0)	3 (0)	1 (0)	0 (0)	0 (0)	6 (0)	3 (1)[c]	1 (0)	44 (3)
Total	79	5	17	10	26	1	109	34	8	309

[a]In addition, in this Parliament Labour dissenters joined with a sufficient number of unwhipped Conservative Members to impose government defeats on six occasions.

[b]Labour Members voting against government during passage of Parliament (No. 2) Bill not included as voting in official Conservative lobby (Opposition whips not being applied in the divisions).

[c]Vote on the principle of entry into the EEC when Labour dissenters entered unwhipped Conservative lobby.

Source: P. Norton, *Dissension in the House of Commons 1974–1979* (Oxford: Oxford University Press, 1980), p. 439.

change need not have been overwhelming in order to be important. . . . We can also appreciate that the decline in parliamentary party cohesion might, like that of the electoral capacity of the major parties, be reversible. But, at least for the 1970s, we must say that the British party model itself substantially changed. A cohesive party as well as a majority party became less certain.[7]

Not only were Members of Parliament prepared to vote against their own side on more occasions and in greater numbers, they were prepared also to do so with greater effect. For the first time in the twentieth century, government backbenchers demonstrated their willingness to enter an Opposition lobby and purposely deny the government a majority. Significantly, the defeats began in the Parliament of 1970–4 in which the Heath government had a clear overall majority. Conservative MPs voted with the Opposition in sufficient numbers to deny the government a majority on six occasions. Three of the six defeats took place on three-line whips, the most important taking place on the immigration rules in November 1972.[8] (On that occasion, the government went down to defeat with a majority of 35 against it, a total of 56 Conservative MPs having cross-voted or abstained). The number of defeats was to be added to significantly in the next two Parliaments.

In the short Parliament of March to October 1974, the minority Labour government was vulnerable to defeat as a result of opposition parties combining against it. After some initial reluctance, opposition parties did prove willing to defeat the government in the division lobbies, doing so on 17 occasions.[9] In the Parliament returned in October 1974, the Labour government was open to defeat as a result of some of its own backbenchers voting against it and as a result (after April 1976 when it lost its overall majority in the House) of opposition parties combining against it. In that Parliament, the government suffered a total of 42 defeats, 23 of them because Labour MPs voted in the Opposition lobby and 19 because opposition parties joined forces against it (see table 2.3). Thus, in the seven-year period from April 1972 (when the defeats began) to April 1979, there was a total of 65 government defeats in the House of Commons' division lobbies. For a similar number of defeats in a seven-year period, one has to go back to the 1860s.

Many of the defeats took place on important issues, the more so as the decade progressed. In the 1974–9 Parliament, the government lost its most important constitutional measure, the Scotland and Wales Bill, following defeat on the guillotine motion for the Bill. The two subsequent Bills, the Scotland Bill and the Wales Bill, were subject to radical amendment as a result of backbench dissent. The provision

Table 2.3   Government defeats in the Commons' division lobbies, 1970–1979

| Parliament | Number of defeats | | |
	Caused by intra-party dissent by government backbenchers	Caused by opposition parties combining against a minority government	Total
1970–4	6	0	6
1974	0	17	17
1974–9	23	19	42
Total	29	36	65

that in a referendum 40 per cent of eligible voters had to vote 'Yes' (otherwise a motion for the repeal of the measure was to be tabled) was inserted in each Bill against the wishes of the government.[10] Another amendment, to exclude the Orkney and Shetland islands from the provisions of the Scotland Bill if a majority of islanders voted 'No' in a referendum, was carried against the government by a majority of 86 votes, 50 Labour Members voting with Conservative and Liberal MPs to ensure its acceptance. The government also suffered the effective wrecking of the Dock Work Regulation Bill as a result of backbench dissent, as well as a change in the basic rate of income tax as a result of a defeat on the 1978 Finance Bill. The government likewise suffered defeats on motions covering its economic policy, Expenditure White Papers and the devaluation of the green pound before its final and definitive defeat on a vote of confidence on 28 March 1979.

Nor were these defeats in the division lobbies the only defeats to be suffered by the government. Throughout the decade, a large number of defeats were inflicted in standing committees. The Heath government of 1970–4 suffered 24 such defeats (more than the combined number to have occurred in the preceding three Parliaments);[11] the Parliament of 1974 witnessed the same number of defeats (24), while in the first four sessions of the 1974–9 Parliament there were approximately a hundred such defeats (97 up to April 1978).[12] These included the so-called Rooker/Wise amendments to the 1977 Finance Bill, which raised the levels of income tax allowances and partially indexed them against inflation. Most of the defeats imposed in standing committee were accepted, wholly or in part, by the Labour government.[13]

A combination of backbench dissent on the floor of the House and in standing committees, at least that which resulted in government defeats, and opposition parties combining against a minority government ensured that a significant proportion of government measures were modified against the government's wishes. Indeed, according to John Schwarz's analysis, more than half the government Bills considered in the 1975-6 session were altered as a result of division-lobby or standing-committee defeats. In the remaining sessions, the proportion of Bills altered ranged from 22 per cent to 45 per cent.[14] The extent of the changes in the Parliament, argued Schwarz, was such as to justify the claim that the House of Commons had acquired a new role in policy-making.

The 1979–83 Parliament

Towards the end of the 1970s, the experience of dissent and, more especially, of government defeats induced a change of attitude towards government on the part of many MPs. Many Members began to take a degree of voting independence for granted.[15] They shed their old deferential attitude towards government in favour of a more participant one.[16] They wanted to be more involved and to have some effect on government measures.

This changed attitude on the part of many Members was to be carried into the new Parliament returned in 1979. It was reflected in Members' continued willingness to dissent from the line taken by their leaders. In this Parliament, though, there were two aspects to the dissent. One was the continued expression of dissent in the division lobbies. The other was the significance of the threat of dissent. Despite the return of a government with a clear overall majority and an Oppsition that was facing difficulties in maintaining cohesion within its own ranks, the government had to contend on occasion with the possibility of defeat. The factors peculiar to the 1974–9 Parliament (a minute and then a non-existent parliamentary majority) were no longer present, but the dissent expressed by government backbenchers, and its effect, was at least on a par with that of the Parliament of 1970–4. There was no reversion to the pre–1970 position of cohesion and guaranteed government majorities.

Let us consider the two aspects of dissent in the Parliament. Throughout the four sessions, there were instances of cross-voting by Conservative backbenchers. Any expectation on the part of government and Opposition whips that they were in for a quiet Parliament was dispelled within the first two months of the opening session. Before the House had recessed for the summer, one in three of all divisions was witnessing dissenting votes cast by one or more Conservative or Labour backbenchers, the dissenters often forcing the divisions themselves.[17] The most significant occasions of Conservative dissent in the Parliament, by vote or abstention, are given in Table 2.4. As that table shows, there were at least 16 occasions when ten or more Conservative MPs either voted against their own side or abstained from voting. On four occasions, the number of dissenters exceeded 40. An examination not only of the numbers involved but also of the government response to the dissent suggests the importance of those occasions. Nonetheless, the number of divisions involved is a very small one, minute in relation to the total number of divisions held in the Parliament (just over 1 per cent of the total). Furthermore, despite the numbers of dissenters involved, on only one occasion did Conservative MPs enter an opposition lobby in sufficient numbers to inflict a defeat on the government (in December 1982 on the immigration rules). Not surprisingly, therefore, some observers have been inclined to dismiss intra-party dissent in the Parliament as of little significance.[18]

More significant, and somewhat overlooked by some students of Parliament, was the threat of defeat. Voting against one's own side in the division lobbies, it should be remembered, constitutes essentially an admission of failure, failure at an earlier stage to persuade one's own leaders not to persist with the measure or motion under debate. If a dissenter is alone in his dissent, or is joined by like-minded Members insufficient in number to threaten the government's majority, then cross-voting may merely serve to confirm that failure. It is at the discretion of government whether or not it chooses to ignore that dissent. What was significant about the 1979 Parliament was that backbenchers proved effective in influencing government *prior* to issues being taken to the division lobbies. Ian Gilmour once observed that 'concord and peace may signify backbench influence, not dull obedience.'[19] The truth of this was borne out to some extent by the experience of this Parliament. Various measures were introduced by a government which did not enjoy the wholehearted support of the parliamentary party. On occasion the number of backbenchers who made it clear to the whips that they were prepared to vote against the government was such as to threaten the government's majority. Rather than run the risk of such defeat, the government conceded the dissenters' point, either wholly or in part. Hence there was little or no dissent in the division lobbies: there was no need for it.

Instances of such pre-lobby dissent are, in one sense, more significant than cross-voting in the division lobbies (at least that which does not entail government defeats) but are, by their nature, less observable. Known instances in the Parliament encompassed two occasions when the government withdrew Bills, a Local Government

Table 2.4 Main occasions of Conservative dissidence in the Commons' division lobbies, 1979–1983

Date	Issue	No. of Conservative MPs dissenting (by vote or abstention)	Comment
11.6.79	Kiribati Bill	15	No effect on Bill
4.12.79	Immigration rules	19	Proposals withdrawn/rules relaxed
11.2.80	Charges for rural school transport	20	Provision withdrawn
23.4.80	Amendment to Employment Bill (on closed shop reform)	42	Backbench proposal incorporated in 1982 Employment Act
5.6.80	Opposition motion calling (in effect) for repeal of so-called 'sus' law	6	Government accepted need for change in law
16.3.81	Increase in petrol duty	28	Increase halved (from 20p to 10p)
7.7.81	Reductions in defence expenditure for naval dockyards	11	No effect
12.11.81	Referendum requirement for local rate increases	18	Proposal abandoned
8.12.81	Public expenditure reductions	14	No immediate tangible effect
9.12.81	Increased weight allowance for heavy lorries	11	Review of Armitage recommendations undertaken
Feb–July 82	5% abatement in real value of unemployment benefit	41[a]	See below
17.6.82	Opposition motion attacking EEC and European Union	9	No effect
23.6.82	Provision for Northern Ireland Assembly	14	No effect
11.11.82	Immigration rules revision	52	Review of immigration quotas undertaken
22.11.82	Abatement in unemployment benefit and abatement in child benefit	25	Abatement restored in March 1983 Budget
25.11.82	Increased weight allowance for heavy lorries	23	No immediate effect
15.12.82	Immigration rules	51	Government defeat. Some tightening of immigration register
15.2.83	Immigration rules	15	No effect

Figures for numbers of dissenters are usually minimum figures, given that they seek to include abstentions.
[a] More than one division involved.

Source: M. Shah, 'Revolts and Retreats: Division Lobby Dissent within the Parliamentary Conservative Party, November 1979–March 1983', unpublished undergraduate dissertation, Essex University Department of Government, 1983; supplemented by author's research of *House of Commons Debates* (*Hansard*).

Finance Bill and the Iran (Temporary Provisions) Bill. In the latter case, a special meeting of senior ministers was called when a Labour MP obtained an emergency debate to discuss the government's plans to introduce the measure. According to *The Times*, as many as 100 Conservative MPs were prepared to vote with the Opposition.[20] The chief whip reported to the meeting that the government faced defeat and the decision was taken to withdraw the measure.[21] In the former case, backbenchers made it clear that they would not accept the provisions for limiting supplementary rates levied by local authorities. The Environment Secretary offered six alternative schemes. None proved acceptable and so the decision was taken to abandon the Bill.[22] Other proposals withdrawn under threat of defeat included charges for eye tests, reductions in the BBC's external services, a three-stage pay rise for MPs (Members opposed the staggered element of the proposal), 'hotel' charges for patients in NHS hospitals, and, in practice, transport charges for school travel in rural areas.[23] Furthermore, the threat of dissent and, more generally, anticipation of likely dissent helped create the broad limits within which the government operated its economic policy. The disquiet prevalent among a section of the parliamentary Conservative party was one of the influences on the Chancellor of the Exchequer in shaping his 1982 Budget. 'Sir Geoffrey Howe', declared *The Economist*, 'may be the first Tory chancellor who, in forming his budget, must take into account his chances of getting it through the House of Commons.'[24] (Twenty-six MPs had earlier written to the chief whip demanding a change of policy; 14 had abstained on the Chancellor's mini-Budget proposals of 2 December the previous year.) In a radio interview early in 1982, the Prime Minister also conceded that she had not been tougher on public spending because of anticipated parliamentary reaction. 'I would like to be tougher on public spending. But I have to do what I think we can get through Parliament.'[25] Though Parliament was only one (and not necessarily the most important) of many influences upon government, it was a more significant one than in pre-1970 days; and in many ways the influence it was exerting was more subtle (and consequently less observable, certainly less quantifiable) than in the preceding Parliaments of the 1970s.

1983: 'The frustration Parliament'?

The position changed significantly in the Parliament returned in June 1983, the result primarily of an overwhelming Conservative presence in the House. The government enjoyed a majority over all other parties of 144. Shortly before the general election, the then Foreign Secretary, Francis Pym, had expressed the view that a large majority would not be a desirable thing. Subsequently, after being relegated to the backbenches, he was to write: 'to put it bluntly, I was right.'[26] Government, he believed, was not capable of being kept in check by a 'tiresome' House of Commons if the House itself was saturated with government supporters.[27] There was the danger also that, with so many Conservative MPs, service in the House for many would prove unrewarding and frustrating, unable to have much impact on government. This view was given some credence by the Speaker when, addressing journalists, he referred to it as the 'frustration Parliament'.

How valid, then, are these observations? What effect, if any, has the House had upon government? Clearly, the effect of a large government majority – the largest since 1945 – has had a significant limiting effect. The government stands little chance of being defeated in the division lobbies in heavily whipped votes. Whereas in the preceding Parliament the threat of cross-voting by 20 or 30 Conservative MPs would have put the government's majority in jeopardy, it would require 70 to 80 Conservative MPs to threaten to cross-vote to achieve a similar result in the present Parliament. The government is thus largely in a position where many believe it can safely ignore its parliamentary critics, be they on the opposition side of the House or its own. To some extent, this is correct; but not wholly, and it is not borne out completely by the evidence of the first session of the Parliament.

A large government majority is assumed to facilitate or rather not to deter backbench critics of the government in casting dissenting votes, because they know that by so voting they can make a point without jeopardizing the government's majority. This assumption was partially borne out by the data on division-lobby dissent in the first session. Indeed, in its occurrence it was more extensive than that experienced in the other two post-war Parliaments with large government majorities (1945–50 and 1959–64), being on a par rather with the incidence of dissent in the preceding Parliaments of the 1970s (table 2.5; compare with table 2.1). The spirit of independence instilled in the 1970s carried over into this Parliament. On the Conservative side of the House, 137 backbenchers cast a total of 416 dissenting votes against the government. The main occasions of dissent are listed in table 2.6. None threatened the government's majority. (In one division on the Rates Bill, the government's majority fell to 21, though there was no cross-voting by Conservative Members.)[28] The extent of the

Table 2.5   Divisions witnessing dissenting votes: June 1983 to summer recess 1984

Number of divisions witnessing dissenting votes			Number of divisions witnessing dissenting votes expressed as a percentage of all division
Total	Lab.[a]	Con.[a]	
115	54	62	25[b]

[a]As one division may witness dissenting votes cast by Conservative *and* Labour Members, the Lab. and Con. figures do not necessarily add up to the total on the left.
[b]When expressed solely as a percentage of all whipped divisions, the figure increases to 28 per cent.

dissent was nonetheless distinctive for the first *session* of the new Parliament.

It was distinctive also for another reason. Despite its extent, it was remarkable that there was not more of it. On a variety of issues, the number of Conservative MPs opposed to the government's proposals was known to be greater than the number actually voting against; examples would include the Rates Bill, housing benefits and the rate support grant for England.[29] In the case of the rate support grant, for instance, at least 20 Conservatives were known originally to be opposed to it; yet in the division only three voted against.[30] On many issues, a majority of dissenters contented themselves with (at most) abstaining from voting. Why? Because the government, though knowing it was not going to be defeated, was prepared to make concessions to avoid the embarrassing display of public, large-scale dissent. The approach adopted was summarized by one journal thus: 'To avoid an open revolt, the chief whip, Mr John Wakeham, would normally seek a negotiated deal between the rebels and the relevant minister before an issue reached the floor of the House. This happened with housing benefit ... as it did with the proposed withholding of Britain's EEC budget contribution.'[31] More often, it recorded, such negotiation did not have the desired effect. Nonetheless, on a number of significant occasions, concession by government served to reduce the scale of dissent.

In the instance of housing benefits, the Social Services Secretary announced in the House that he was prepared to consider modifying his own proposals if they looked like having a harsh effect on some households;[23] he was also reported to have given some privately expressed assurances to the backbench dissenters.[33] Concessions were

Table 2.6 Main occasions of Conservative dissidence in the Commons' division lobbies, 1983/4 session

Date	Issue	Number of Conservative MPs voting against government (Number of abstainers, where known, given in parenthesis)
1.12.83	Opposition amendment 'that the own resources of the European Community should not be increased'	6 (17)
17.1.84	Rates Bill: Second Reading	12 (20/30)
17.1.84	Rates Bill: motion to commit to Committee of the Whole House	20
19.1.84	Opposition motion urging government to reconsider changes in housing benefits	3 (5/10)
23.1.84	Rate Support Grant for England 1984/5	3 (c.10)
27/28.3.84	Rates Bill: various amendments	14
28.3.84	Rates Bill: Third Reading	9 (10/20)
2.4.84	Trade Union Bill: amendment to require 'contracting in' for paying political levy	43
11.4.84	Local Government (Interim Provisions) Bill: Second Reading	19 (10/20)
2.5.84	Health and Social Security Bill: amendment re safeguards in dispensing of glasses by non-registered opticians	10
9/10.5.84	Local Government (Interim Provisions) Bill: various amendments	22
14.5.84	Police and Criminal Evidence Bill: amendment to provide that police officers had to be in uniform to arrest under the 1956 Sexual Offences Act	7
6.6.84	Agricultural Holdings Bill: new clause (waiver of contract)	5 (1+)
13.6.84	Matrimonial and Family Proceedings Bill: amendment to allow solicitors to appear in family court proceedings	5
24.7.84	Trade Union Bill: various amendments	37

Sources: House of Commons Debates (Hansard) for data on cross-voting; national press for reports of abstentions.

also forthcoming on the Rates Bill and EC milk-production regulations. On the Rates Bill, the Environment Secretary announced that the Bill would be amended to exempt from general rate-capping powers those authorities which had followed government spending guidelines.[34] As one backbench critic declared, 'It goes a long way . . . to make the Bill much more acceptable.'[35] The government withdrew the EC milk-production regulations it had originally tabled, substituting instead regulations that were somewhat more satisfactory to dairy farmers and backbench critics.[36] Ministers also moved to make conciliatory gestures in anticipation of dissent on other issues, including the Police and Criminal Evidence Bill and the rate support grant.[37] Anticipated disquiet on the backbenches also affected Cabinet discussion on a number of issues, including a Treasury proposal for a freeze on capital spending by local authorities. It was resisted by Environment Secretary Patrick Jenkin. 'Mr Jenkin has been given ample warning in recent weeks that a freeze would encounter the deepest hostility from Conservative as well as Labour councils as well as from Tory backbench MPs. . . . Many of Mr Jenkin's ministerial colleagues at last night's meeting share his belief that the Government would be foolhardy to alienate them further.'[38]

Thus on occasion backbenchers were able to persuade government to make concessions, in some instances concessions of some substance. In so doing, they lacked the clout that flows from being able to threaten the government's majority in the lobbies. But they were aided by developments elsewhere – in the 'other place'. Government appears to have been influenced by the occasional axis developed between dissident Conservative MPs and the Upper House. The behavioural changes identified by Nicholas Baldwin in chapter 5 – peers being willing to use their power to defeat the government on a number of issues – not only embarrassed the government but also provided backbench critics with additional leverage. The government could confidently seek to reverse Lords' amendments if it had a united parliamentary party behind it. If it did not, seeking a reversal could produce not a defeat but further serious embarrassment, exploited by both the Opposition and dissident backbenchers alike. Hence, in many respects, for government the 'opposition' that caused it most concern was not the official Opposition but instead the combined opposition of Lords and dissident backbenchers.

Relative to preceding Parliaments, MPs were able to wring fewer concessions out of government than they would likely have wished. Nonetheless they were able to have some, however limited, impact upon government deliberations (the Prime Minister, as one occasional dissident put it, 'remained a good listener'),[39] and the more independent spirit generated in the 1970s was still apparent. Indeed, this independent spirit was marked on those issues which are by tradition considered House of Commons matters and on those considered issues of conscience. On the selection of the Speaker, Members made it clear that they were unwilling to support the Member preferred by the Prime Minister, making sure that the appointment went instead to Bernard Weatherill (an MP, for some reason, out of favour with the Prime Minister). On the issue of MPs' pay, Members failed in one division to go along with government advice (in the division, government whips acting as tellers, the vote went against government advice by 233 votes to 160).[40] And in a series of divisions on capital punishment, a conscience issue, a majority of Members voted consistently against its reintroduction, despite both the Prime Minister and the Home Secretary voting for it.[41]

There were clearly significant differences between the Parliaments in the three periods identified. However, there was one generalization that was no longer appropriate to any of them. At the beginning of the chapter, two generalizations appropriate to pre-1970 Parliaments were identified: MPs rarely voted against their own side, and when they did so they did not deny the government a majority. This latter generalization (not defeating the government) was not borne out by the Parliaments of the 1970s and that of 1979–83, but would seem applicable again to the present Parliament. The first generalization, however, applies to none of the Parliaments covered. Expressed in sheer behavioural terms (that is, ignoring the impact or otherwise of such behaviour), Members of Parliament have proved significantly more willing since 1970 to vote against their own party in the division lobbies. As one MP expressed it, by the late 1970s Members were taking a degree of voting independence for granted.[42] The change is relative – cohesion remains a feature of the division lobbies – but it is significant. Two questions then arise. What explains this sudden upsurge in parliamentary intra-party dissent? And what effect has it had?

Explanations of Change

Dissent does not occur in a vacuum. In the late 1960s and in the 1970s, government in Britain was finding itself faced with increasing and to some observers near-insuperable economic problems. Various issues were coming or had come on to the agenda of political debate that were not congruent with traditional party stances, most notably that of British membership of the European Communities. Yet these developments by themselves, while they may help explain why Members disagreed with their own front benches (opposition to changing economic policy, or to EC entry), do not necessarily explain why Members were prepared to express their dissent in the *form* that they did, i.e. in the division lobbies, nor why that form of expression showed such a dramatic increase in the first Parliament of the 1970s. After all, the economic problems encountered by the nation in the wake of the Second World War were greater than those of the early 1970s and the issue of British membership of the European Economic Community had come on to the agenda of debate during the Macmillan premiership. Yet the willingness of MPs to vote against their own side was significantly greater in the 1970–4 Parliament than it had been in the Parliaments of 1945–50 and 1959–64 (see table 2.1). Why? The explanation, I would contend, is to be found in the prime ministerial leadership of Edward Heath.

As Prime Minister, Mr Heath was concerned primarily to ensure that the measures his government introduced were not only passed, but passed in the form in which they were introduced. Enacting the government's programme took priority over maintaining unity within the parliamentary party. (Indeed, to many, the government's programme was in effect Mr Heath's programme. Lord John Russell once said of Sir Robert Peel: 'I treat him as if he were the government – as he is in the habit of treating himself.' Much the same could be said of Mr Heath.) The Prime Minister's stubbornness in insisting on the passage of legislation without conceding any amendments of substance impelled many Conservative MPs who disagreed with that legislation to express their disagreement in public, authoritative form – in the division lobbies. As already observed, cross-voting in the division lobbies is usually a sign of failure, a sign that attempts to influence government at an earlier stage have been fruitless. This was notably the case in this 1970–4 Parliament. Furthermore, a willingness to dissent was facilitated by other facets of Mr Heath's leadership style. He was not disposed to garner support among backbenchers either by recourse to developing personal friendships (he was considered cold and aloof by most backbenchers and had a reputation for snubbing those who had disagreed with some aspect of government policy) or at the intellectual level by explaining policies, especially changes in policy. Once a decision was made, he expected the parliamentary party to support it. He had also a distaste for judicious (that is, in a way to encourage a more contented attitude on the part of Members ambitious for office or honours) use of his powers of appointment and patronage. These features coalesced to produce a leadership style which became increasingly resented by backbenchers and which made them more willing, on those occasions when they disagreed with the government, to express their dissent in the division lobbies.[43] Certainly, Mr Heath (and some of those around him) appeared to appreciate towards the very end of his period as party leader the effect his leadership style was having on backbenchers; too late, though, to save him being deprived of that leadership.[44] Ironically, by the most forceful exercise of prime ministerial leadership in recent times, Edward Heath precipitated a significant increase in backbench independence – and his own ejection from the leadership of the Conservative Party.

No other explanation for the upsurge in Conservative *division-lobby* dissent in the 1970–4 Parliament is as plausible as that of Mr Heath's style of prime ministerial leadership. The increase in cross-voting cannot be attributed to the political disquiet generated by economic problems consequent to the oil crisis of 1973 nor to the return of minority and near-minority governments in 1974. The increase in cross-voting preceded both events. Both may have helped facilitate dissent, and more effective dissent, in the latter half of the decade but they were not the initial cause of it. Other explanations offered have included those of ideology and a 'new breed of MP' being returned, more willing to dissent from the party leadership in the division lobbies.[45] Neither is borne out by the empirical evidence. There was an ideological base to *some* of the dissent expressed in the Parliament, Enoch Powell providing a focus for neo-liberals opposed to the government's economic, industrial and European policies.[46] But ideology does not provide an exclusive or comprehensive explanation of dissent in the Parliament; and studies of Conservative cross-voting in later Parliaments have found no ideological base to explain the extent of that cross-voting.[47] Nor (unlike the experience of the Labour government in the 1974–9 Parliaments)[48] could the dissent be attributed to a new breed of MP entering the House. In two of the three Parliaments of Conservative government (1970–4 and that of 1983–) the new intake of Conservative MPs has provided neither the leaders of dissent nor a disproportionate number of cross-voters; if anything, the reverse.[49] Nor have the new Members been responsible indirectly, through precipitating a change in Members' role perceptions; new MPs in the 1970s apparently resembled old MPs in their attitudes to party loyalty.[50] The one variable that does explain the sudden upsurge in cross-voting in the 1970–4 Parliament and why in the 1979 and 1983 Parliaments the extent of cross-voting has been less than the number of known dissenters is that of leadership style.

Mr Heath was not prepared to compromise. By contrast, Mrs Thatcher and her government have been prepared to offer concessions on a number of sometimes significant issues. It is highly unlikely that Mr Heath would have been prepared to countenance such concessions even if threatened with defeat. He tended to push on regardless, even if advised by his chief whip, Francis Pym, that the government might not have a majority. Mrs Thatcher has adopted a leadership style notably at variance (and deliberately so) with that of her predecessor. 'Mr Heath was . . . a stern, puritanical Prime Minister in a way that Mrs Thatcher has turned out not to be'.[51] Public impressions notwithstanding, she has been careful to try to maintain her contact with backbenchers. She has tried to ensure that she dines regularly at the Commons with Conservative MPs. She has made it a practice to have periodic meetings with officers of backbench party committees.[52] Her distribution of honours 'is, if anything, now being noted for being too lavish'.[53] These features, added to the willingness on occasion to concede points, have served to discourage Members from going more often into the division lobbies against the wishes of the whips. Members themselves are conscious of the fact that, though unable to defeat the government, they are nonetheless able to gain the ear of the relevant minister or, if needs be, the Prime Minister.[54] There are indications that Mrs Thatcher, emboldened by a large majority, may be changing her leadership style. If that is the case, it is likely to result in backbench dissent being expressed more often and in the more authoritative forum of the division lobbies. The change in attitude generated by the experience of the 1970s has not been dispelled. The government's majority may not be threatened, but the unity of its parliamentary party can no longer be taken for granted. The roots of this change are to be found in Edward Heath's leadership style. That triggered off behaviour that created a precedent for further changes in the latter half of the 1970s, changes that were to be encouraged by fortuitous developments – most notably the results of the 1974 general elections. The consequence was to be the significant modification in voting behaviour sketched above. Cohesion, as already noted, still remains a feature of parliamentary life, but it is no longer the overwhelming, consistent and hence predictable cohesion that was prevalent in the period from 1945 to 1970.

The Effects of Dissent

There was, then, a sharp increase in cross-voting in the Commons' division lobbies in the 1970s. The incidence of division-lobby dissent in the present Parliament has been on a par with that of preceding Parliaments. Yet, whatever the reasons for it, does it matter? Has it had an appreciable effect? The answer, I would contend, is in the affirmative. It has had an effect in three significant respects.

First, important from the perspective of the student of politics as well as the parliamentarian, it has served to dispel many previously held assumptions about parliamentary behaviour and about a pre-sumed constitutional convention. The assumption prevalent among MPs (and not discouraged by ministers and whips) that every division was tantamount virtually to a vote of confidence in the government and that therefore a defeat on an important issue (indeed on any issue according to some writers) would necessitate the government resigning or requesting a dissolution was shown to amount to no more than a constitutional myth. It was an assumption with no basis in past practice or in any authoritative original source.[55] The string of defeats in the 1970s, in response to which the government of the day acted in line with nineteenth- and twentieth-century precedents, demonstrated the hollowness of the assumption. In so doing it served to remove what had previously been an important constraint on Members' voting behaviour; so long as government backbenchers had believed the assertion they had restrained their dissenting voting behaviour accordingly. The experience of dissent revealed also that the whips were not the wielders of great disciplinary sanctions, able to bring great powers to bear against rebellious backbenchers. Indeed, Members began to realize that the whips had little effective power other than that of persuasion. As one Conservative whip expressed the position: 'We have no powers of sanction; I mean, if a Member of Parliament says he's not going to do anything, well, he jolly well doesn't do it and there's nothing I can do about it, I can't bribe him.'[56] There was a growing awareness and appreciation of the fact that the essential tasks of the whips were those of communication and management, not of discipline.[57] Dissent throughout the 1970s also led to a growing realization that voting against one's own side on important issues was not necessarily a bar to promotion (ability was a far more significant criterion than voting behaviour)[58] and that constituency parties, though by far the most important constraint in practice on a Member's behaviour, did not provide the political straitjacket that many observers – and MPs – had presumed that they did. Members running into trouble with their constituency parties on the basis of parliamentary cross-voting were usually readopted to contest the next election.[59] Members vulnerable to the charge of neglecting their constituencies were far more likely to be challenged effectively. The realization that such presumed constraints were not quite as effective as previously assumed had important implications for parliamentary behaviour. Once such assumptions – about the power of the whips, government reaction to defeat and so on – have been dispelled, it is difficult to resuscitate them.

Second, there was the direct and sometimes observable impact that dissent had and continues to have on public policy. As we have seen, as a result either of defeat in the division lobbies, or the threat of defeat, or sometimes of dissent not entailing defeat, government has modified and sometimes withdrawn measures. Some of the modifications have been essentially minor, especially when set against the totality of public policy. Others have been significant, affecting economic policy and (in 1974–9) the major constitutional Bill of a Labour government. Such has been the extent and importance of backbench dissent that anticipation of it has become important in ministerial deliberations, not only in the 1970s but also, as we have observed, during Mrs Thatcher's premiership. Though the House never achieved anything approaching the policy-making role claimed for it by John Schwarz, it became a relatively more significant policy-influencing body. That significance was most marked during the 1970s and in the Parliament of 1979–83 when the House essentially was able to force its will on government, either through defeat in the lobbies or through the threat of defeat. That sanction is not readily available in the present Parliament, but the government has nonetheless made concessions in the face of threatened dissent; to that extent, therefore, influence has been exerted. Whatever happens in the future, the fact that Parliament has had and, to a lesser extent, continues to have some influence upon public policy cannot be discounted. It remains one of many influences upon policy but an influence nonetheless; and that influence has been greater in the period since 1970 than it was in the post-war years from 1945 to 1970 – greater, indeed, than in pre-war years. As already noted, to discover the same number of defeats as occurred in the seven-year period from 1972 to 1979 one has to go back to the 1860s.

Third, and of long-term significance, the behavioural and attitudinal changes of the 1970s generated the creation of the new departmentally related select committees (discussed by Stephen Downs in chapter 3) and other structural and procedural changes (identified in appendix 1). Previously, the initiative for reform, for creating new select committees, rested with government, principally the Leader of the House. The reforms of the latter half of the 1960s were dubbed the 'Crossman reforms': Richard Crossman proposed them and they became associated with his name. Just as the onus for creating new committees rested with government, so it felt confident in doing away with such reforms when it so wished. Select committees, in their creation and their continuation, were thus in a sense the creatures of government. This was to change in the latter half of the 1970s. The Select Committee on Procedure in its 1978 report recommended the creation of a comprehensive set of select committees to scrutinize the activities of the main departments of state.[60] The then Leader of the House, Michael Foot, was opposed to the report and sought to ignore it. However, it found favour with Members on both sides of the House and they in effect forced Mr Foot to concede a debate on it. Members were no longer prepared to defer to government on what were essentially House of Commons matters. Having achieved a debate, they then demanded that a vote on the committee's recommendations be arranged. As one report observed:

Is Parliament's control of the executive ever destined to ebb remorselessly away? MPs were inclined this week to answer no, when they forced an unwilling Government to concede them the chance to decide whether major changes should be made in parliamentary procedure. . . . when Government decided that this report should merely be debated but not voted on they reacted angrily. . . . the Government was made to promise that there will be a vote sometime. . . . MPs were in no mood to be fobbed off. Support for the proposals and demand for a vote came from all sides of the House.[61]

The 1979 general election then intervened. A debate on the committee's recommendations was soon arranged and on 25 June 1979 the House, by a vote of 248 to 12, approved the creation of the new select committees. The committees were, then, as much the creation of the House as of the government; indeed, the incoming Conservative Cabinet was at best lukewarm towards the proposals, some Cabinet ministers either being hostile (a category that included the Prime Minister) or at best indifferent. The House is thus the body that has been prepared to take a lead both in establishing and in sustaining the committees. It was the House also that ensured that the National Audit Act, introduced as a Private Member's Bill by Norman St John-Stevas, was enacted.[62] The Bill, which sought the creation of the National Audit Office and a Public Accounts Commission, was opposed by the government. However, the strength of support for the Bill in the House was such that the government was forced to compromise and the Bill was passed shortly before the House was prorogued in 1983.

The behavioural changes of the 1970s thus made possible the creation of a new committee structure – of a qualitatively as well as quantitatively different nature to previous such structures – and other structural and procedural reforms. The departmentally related select committees are now an established feature of the parliamentary landscape. The Leader of the House, John Biffen, has conceded that they now have the characteristics of a permanent system; he could not envisage their demise.[63] The Public Accounts Commission, manned by nine MPs, constitutes a statutory as opposed to a parliamentary committee.[64] Thus, regardless of whether the behavioural changes of recent years prove to be lasting, they have served to generate structures, for the regular scrutiny of government, which are permanent.

Conclusion

The House of Commons, in its behaviour, has changed a great deal since 1970. Members of Parliament have proved significantly more willing to vote against their own side. They have also proved willing, for most of this period, to do so in such numbers as to threaten or remove the government's majority on a number of occasions. Cohesion remains a feature of parliamentary voting, but it is not the cohesion of the pre-1970 era. Party leaders can no longer take their parliamentary parties for granted. Relative to preceding Parliaments (i.e. pre-1970) MPs have become more independent in their voting behaviour, an independence which has been maintained in the present Parliament returned in 1983. By indulging in such behaviour, Members have served to dispel a number of assumptions previously held about the House of Commons, they have served to make the House a more significant policy-*influencing* body (though the extent of that influence has varied from Parliament to Parliament, depending upon MPs' willingness and ability to deny the government a majority in the division lobbies), and they have served to generate parliamentary structures for subjecting government to more regular and sustained scrutiny. Though the House has not achieved anything approaching the policy-making role ascribed to it by some observers, to write – as Beer does – of 'the rise of Parliament' in the 1970s is probably not inappropriate. What one is now witnessing is a period of consolidation.

The government's large majority in the House provides a barrier to the House exerting greater or as much policy influence as it did in the 1970s; but the select committees created by the House in 1979 are now in established operation and, according to some of their members, operating more smoothly and with at least as much effect as in the first Parliament of their existence. Thus the behavioural changes of recent years are important both for the effect they had at the time and for their long-term implications. Because of them, the House of Commons is unlikely to revert to being quite the same animal that it was in the decades prior to 1970.

Notes

1 S. H. Beer, *Modern British Politics* (London: Faber, 1969 edition), pp. 350–1.
2 Ibid.
3 S. H. Beer, *Britain Against Itself* (London: Faber, 1982), p. 181.
4 Ibid. Beer uses the phrase as the heading for the section on Parliament.
5 J. E. Schwarz, 'Exploring a New Role in Policy-making: The British House of Commons in the 1970s', *American Political Science Review*, 74(1), March 1980, pp. 23–37.
6 P. Norton, *Dissension in the House of Commons 1974–1979* (Oxford: Oxford University Press, 1980), p. 437.
7 L. D. Epstein, 'What Happened to the British Party Model?' *American Political Science Review*, 74(1), 1980, pp. 19–20.
8 See P. Norton, 'Intra-party Dissent in the House of Commons: A Case Study. The Immigration Rules 1972', *Parliamentary Affairs*, 29(4), 1976, pp. 404–20.
9 See Norton, *Dissension in the House of Commons 1974–1979*, p. 491.
10 See ibid., pp. 310–12, 327–9 and 345–6.
11 P. Norton, 'Dissent in Committee: Intra-party Dissent in Commons' Standing Committees 1959–74', *The Parliamentarian*, 57(1), 1976, table 1, p. 18.
12 Schwarz, 'Exploring a New Role in Policy-making', table 3, p. 27.
13 Ibid., pp. 27–8.
14 Ibid., table 3, p. 27.
15 Note the comments of G. Cunningham MP, book review, *The Parliamentarian*, 61, 1980, pp. 192–3.
16 Beer, *Britain Against Itself*, p. 190.
17 Of 82 divisions held prior to the summer recess, 60 were whipped on the government side. In 19 divisions, backbenchers forced the vote. In eight of these, Conservative backbenchers were to be found voting against the government.

18 As, for example, in D. Judge (ed.), *The Politics of Parliamentary Reform* (London: Heinemann, 1983), pp. 188–9.
19 I. Gilmour, *The Body Politic* (London: Hutchinson, revised edition 1971), p. 269.
20 *The Times*, 20 May 1980.
21 BBC Radio 4 Programme, 'Today', 20 May 1980.
22 *The Economist*, 19 December 1981.
23 The proposal had encountered cross-voting when it first went through the Commons and had then been defeated in the Lords (see chapter 5). Conservative opposition to the proposal increased (influenced by constituency pressure) and it appeared that the government might not be able to muster a Commons' majority to reverse the Lords' amendment. It was therefore decided not to try to overturn the Lords' decision.
24 *The Economist*, 16 January 1982.
25 Quoted in *The Times*, 11 January 1982.
26 F. Pym, *The Politics of Consent* (London: Hamish Hamilton, 1984), p. 78.
27 Ibid.
28 On 26 June 1984. *HC Deb*. 62, cols 859–62.
29 See *Financial Times*, 29 March 1984; *Daily Telegraph*, 24 January 1984; and *Financial Times*, 20 January 1984.
30 *Daily Telegraph*, 24 January 1984.
31 *The Economist*, 4 August 1984, p. 22.
32 *HC Deb*, 52, cols 465, 471.
33 *Daily Telegraph*, 20 January 1984.
34 *HC Deb*, 57, cols 326–7.
35 *HC Deb*. 57, col. 328.
36 The new regulations allowed for more production by farmers who had entered into commitments before 2 April 1984 and who were unable to obtain sufficient quotas to sustain their businesses. *The Times*, 12 July 1984.
37 On the Police and Criminal Evidence Bill, Home Office ministers sought to reduce support for a Liberal amendment – requiring police officers making arrests under the 1956 Sexual Offences Act to be in uniform – by announcing a tightening of Metropolitan Police rules to ensure that plainclothes officers were not used as *agents provocateurs*. (There was pressure from many Members for such an announcement following an incident in a Soho gay theatre involving the arrest of a Conservative MP by a plainclothes officer. See *Daily Telegraph*, 15 May 1984.) More generally, backbench opinion and anticipated reaction had had an influence in the revision of the Bill, following the loss of the original Bill with the calling of the 1983 general election: Home Secretary Leon Brittan QC, MP to author in interview.
38 *The Times*, 11 July 1984.
39 Robin Maxwell-Hyslop MP addressing students from Hull University, House of Commons, 7 March 1984.

40 *HC Deb.* 46, cols 344–6.

41 *HC Deb*, 45, cols 972–96.

42 G. Cunningham MP; see above note 15.

43 P. Norton, *Conservative Dissidents* (London: Temple Smith, 1978). See especially chapter 9.

44 When his leadership came into question, he tried to draw critics into his fold by offering them front-bench positions; each offer was declined. Once a leadership contest was under way, Mr Heath sought to be more friendly with backbenchers, inviting them to meet him for drinks and the like. 'Bit late for that, isn't it?' commented one Member in response to such an invitation.

45 See D. Marsh, 'Dr Norton's Parliament', *Public Administration Bulletin*, 41, April 1983, pp. 37–8.

46 Norton, *Conservative Dissidents*, pp. 244–54.

47 M. Shah, 'Revolts and Retreats: Division Lobby Dissent within the Parliamentary Conservative Party, Nov. 1979 – March 1983', unpublished undergraduate dissertation, Essex University Department of Government, 1983; author's research of the division lists for the 1983/4 session (up to the summer recess); R. Butt, 'Thatcherism: Living for the Moment', *The Times*, 19 January 1984; and 'Tory Backbenchers: Mutiny in the Sergeants' Mess', *The Economist*, 4 August 1984, p. 22.

48 S. P. Longstreet, 'Rebellion in the Parliamentary Labour Party 1974–1979: A Quantitative Analysis', unpublished PhD thesis, University of Essex, 1984.

49 Author's research of division lists 1970–4 Parliament and 1983/84 session of the 1983 Parliament; see also P. Riddell in *Financial Times*, 25 January 1984, and M. Rutherford, 'The Tories: Still Quite Happy', *Financial Times*, 27 January 1984. In the 1979–83 Parliament, new Members were more prone to cross-vote than longer-serving Members: Shah, 'Revolts and Retreats', pp. 8–9.

50 Based on analysis of survey data of MPs, held by Donald Searing at the University of North Carolina; from an as yet unpublished manuscript by Ed Crowe.

51 Rutherford, 'The Tories.'

52 P. Norton, 'Party Committees in the House of Commons', *Parliamentary Affairs*, 36(1), Winter 1983, p. 14.

53 Rutherford, 'The Tories'.

54 Ibid.

55 P. Norton, 'Government Defeats in the House of Commons: Myth and Reality', *Public Law*, Winter 1978, pp. 360–78.

56 B. Weatherill MP, in a Radio 3 programme, 'The Parliamentary Process: Parties and Parliament', 12 February 1976.

57 See especially P. Norton, 'The Organisation of Parliamentary Parties', in S. A. Walkland (ed.), *The House of Commons in the Twentieth Century* (Oxford: Oxford University Press, 1979), pp. 10–21.

59 See ibid., pp. 466–8 and Norton, *Conservative Dissidents*, ch. 6.
60 *First Report from the Select Committee on Procedure, Session 1977/78*, HC 588 (London: HMSO, 1978).
61 'Parliament Prepares to Seize Power', *The Economist*, 24 February 1979, pp. 23–4.
62 The Bill was introduced as the Parliamentary Control of Expenditure (Reform) Bill. On the initial clash between the House and the Cabinet, see *The Sunday Times*, 9 January 1983.
63 Addressing a seminar held at the Policy Studies Institute, London, on 5 June 1984.
64 The same status attaches to the House of Commons Commission. See appendix 1.

3

Structural Changes
Select Committees: Experiment and Establishment

Stephen J. Downs

This chapter examines one of the main procedural devices employed by the House of Commons to help it meet modern pressures and requirements. Parliament's main task – as detailed in the Introduction – remains that of scrutinizing both legislation and government activity, but in an age when much doubt has been cast upon the abilities of legislatures generally to carry out this role, select committees have been widely advocated for the House of Commons as the modern answer: an efficient and specialist method of probing administration and policy. Our purpose here is to chart the development of these committees from temporary, almost reluctant experiments to the established role they play today.

After many years of procedural dithering, and much controversy, the first full 'system' of select committees was established in the House of Commons in 1979. Each of the 14 new committees has been assigned the responsibility of monitoring a major area of government policy, although in practice they are usually associated with one main 'client' department. To their advocates, they represent a new opportunity for backbenchers from all parties to exert a more continuous, vigorous scrutiny over each important sector of governmental activity. To cynics, their power to send for 'persons, papers and records', backed only by a right to offer 'recommendations' to the House and Government, limits their influence, offering them no real power and relegating them to a peripheral role in the political system. To traditional parliamentarians, their operations are either negligible or a threat to the workings of the Chamber as the 'Grand Forum' for political debate. It would seem that, despite their relative permanence after 1979, the arguments over their role will continue.

If it is accepted that Parliament's major role is to scrutinize and make accountable the actions of the executive, then it must be stipulated at the outset that select committees represent only an additional mechanism of scrutiny designed to complement the overall work of the House through their enquiries and reporting. They are not designed to replace the Chamber as the main focus of parliamentary activity, nor do they possess the power fundamentally to alter the existing nature of the relationship between Parliament and government. They seek to improve the accountability of government to Parliament.

Select committees are a specialized reaction to an overcrowded legislative timetable, to the apparent dominance and growing powers of government, and to an increasingly expert civil service. They offer backbench MPs an opportunity to conduct regular and wide-ranging enquiries before reporting back to the House. Yet they still reflect to some degree the party-oriented nature of their parent body and they remain subject to a similar range of limitations and constraints. So much rhetoric has surrounded their establishment, so many assumptions have been aired regarding their power and effectiveness, that the problems and benefits generated by their operations require very careful assessment before their impact upon the political process can be measured. This chapter attempts to correct some long-held presumptions, to remind readers of the real nature of committee work, and to place the work of select committees in proper perspective.

Assessing Committees

Just what is a 'committee'? More importantly, what makes a good committee, and how closely do the select committees of the House approximate to the ideal? The term 'committee' usually conveys a number of images, not all of them distinct. The referral of a matter to a committee normally implies that a small body has been established to assess a given problem and report accordingly. The ideal image is of a co-ordinated, expert investigative mechanism, and the decision to employ a committee often implies that a larger, possibly more unwieldy body has entrusted to it the power to investigate and then to report to that higher body. At a simplistic level, the powers and responsibilities of a committee would thus appear to be fairly straightforward; it is required to investigate a particular issue or area in the hope that it will produce material of sufficient quality to enhance and expedite the work of a higher and presumably more powerful body.

Unfortunately, the very establishment of a committee, with a *delegated* responsibility to carry out a task, automatically raises a number of problems, all associated with the relationship between a committee and the institution or institutions to which it is responsible. Put simply, if a committee is given the power to investigate and offer recommendations, how much power should this entail and to what extent should a committee *expect* to influence the decisions of its parent body? This is a thorny issue with which the House of Commons and successive governments have grappled during their deliberations on whether or not the House needed some form of select-committee structure. As benefits the age-old and quirky 'Mother of Parliaments', not only did it take a considerable period of time before a full and permanent set of such committees was established, but their powers remain unsure and cloudy, dependent upon their ability to 'influence' but not 'control' the actions of the executive. *Their influence relies not upon sanctions or threats but normally upon the expertise and cogency of their investigations and reporting, and upon how far government is prepared to accede to 'mere' recommendations.*

The House of Commons has two sets of committee, standing and select. Standing committees are used to examine bills, i.e. proposed legislation, clause by clause, before returning them to the House for further consideration and Third Reading. These committees are staffed according to the political complexion of the House and the whipping system operates. Thus, when a vote is taken, the government of the day is *normally* assured of a majority. The reasons for this are the same as on the floor of the House; MPs ordinarily support the policies of their party and are reluctant to vote against their side, both for political and strategic reasons. As Philip Norton has already pointed out, the incidence of backbench dissent, usually in the form of abstention, has increased markedly since 1970, but nevertheless MPs will rebel only reluctantly. Standing committees are *ad hoc* and therefore temporary bodies, each one established purely to examine one particular Bill before being disbanded. Although MPs with an interest in the proposed work of a standing committee are traditionally allocated to serve, the temporary nature of their deliberations precludes the establishment of a long-term investigative role and the development of a corporate identity. Standing committees can and do amend Bills, but these amendments are usually minor; procedure prohibits amendments which challenge the principle of any Bill.

Select committees are obviously different in their role and remit. Yet they are also strangely similar, since it is party politicians who staff them. They were established to scrutinize the policy and administrative practice of particular areas of governmental activity. They do not, for the moment, consider legislation as part of their normal functions. They are given the task of examining topics within their ambit, collecting information and issuing reports. But in order to report they normally must reach conclusions, and in order to reach conclusions politicians from different parties must 'agree' at some level. Select committees too are staffed according to party numbers in the House, so their political complexion is all-important. The incumbent government enjoys a majority in each one. Select committees are different from standing committees in their operations in that, firstly, the whips are removed, and secondly, MPs in their quest for information are presumed somehow to forget or fudge party affiliations. Their 'crusade' against the inadequacies of the executive should presumably lend to their work some form of corporate spirit to enable their enquiries to be pursued with definite direction. How successfully the members of a select committee 'gel' is an important point. Participation on a select committee is thought to offer a backbench MP the opportunity rationally to assess the information he is presented with, distanced to some degree from the overt party struggles of the Chamber and standing committee. But political opinion still plays an important part in their operations: without arguments and differences the proceedings of a committee would be very dull indeed. Compromise may prove possible, but it is not always desirable, nor necessary. Indeed, the best reports are not always give-and-take affairs, but sometimes those which have managed to capture the spirit of challenge amongst members.

Another vital aspect of their rôle concerns their powers. They should act both as 'access points' for those interest groups concerned with a particular issue or area, e.g. defence, and as information-seekers on their own behalf. The gathering of as much relevant information as possible is crucial to their success: they have been granted the power to send for 'persons, papers and records', an all-embracing and rather ambiguous phrase, and although a number of the committees are well supplied with information from groups outside central government circles, the traditional 'enemy' has always been the civil service and government ministers. But this is not always so: committees often enjoy a fruitful relationship with Whitehall. Nevertheless, it has taken some little time before select committees have had their power to summon government witnesses explicitly recognized. It is now a convention that all ministers and civil servants invited to give evidence should attend. Indeed, it is a serious political offence for a minister deliberately to avoid attendance.

However, the presence of witnesses does not automatically mean the provision of information. Some government information will always remain out of bounds. Committees recognize this; for example, the present Defence Committee accepts the existence of sensitive areas and does not pry too deeply into them. But, in common with all the committees, it knows that all other subjects are potentially open to investigation. Nonetheless, the conventions surrounding ministerial responsibility and the general aura of secrecy around Whitehall still present the committees with problems, for there is no concrete requirement that they should be provided information on demand. Different committees have different records regarding the extraction of information which was previously withheld. The provision of information, bearing in mind that these committees are charged with 'finding out', is still a major constitutional sticking-point.[1]

Nor can the committees be sure that their recommendations will be carried out. They can suggest, recommend, protest, demand, but once they have reported the extent of their impact depends very much upon the issue they have covered, upon whether it is politically interesting or topical, upon whether backbench MPs are attracted to their findings, and most importantly, upon the reactions of ministers. Once a report is issued, it represents just another document in a field of many. If it avoids gathering dust on the shelf, it might with luck be allotted a debate in the House (reports are not automatically debated – to date, only 3 per cent of reports have been), or support for its findings might gather momentum in the inexplicable way that they often do. Depending upon how far the recommendations challenge the government's existing policies, the report might even enjoy some success, in either the short or the long term, as just one of the many pressures which lead up to a particular course of action.

Another major aspect of the work of select committees concerns their membership, for the extent to which they can demonstrate expertise and a sense of permanence determines how much legitimacy and force their proceedings and findings will have. In the past, problems of recruitment had hindered the development of committees, but nowadays MPs *want* to sit on select committees. Vacant seats are usually oversubscribed. (In the last Parliament, for example, 80 members applied for two vacancies on the Defence Committee.) But for an MP to specialize in a particular area of public policy rests upon what David Judge terms the 'mix' of interests which they are prepared to take upon themselves.[2] Since select committees are only one set of cogs in a very large machine, MPs must combine their interests and commitments. Most MPs today have a very crowded schedule and adopt a more professional attitude to their work, in contrast to the 'gentlemen amateurs' of the past. But MPs are first and foremost politicians, with a variety of interests, pressures and duties, and this limits their ability to specialize and their commitment to committee work. However, a large number of MPs, particularly the chairmen of the new committees, are becoming recognized as specialists and/or committee men. (Notable examples include Terence Higgins – and formerly Edward du Cann – of the Treasury Committee; Sir Anthony Kershaw of Foreign Affairs; and John Wheeler of the Home Affairs sub-committee.) The Members attracted to select-committee service are usually either well versed in the subject, or keen to learn. Committee work thus forms an important part of the learning process for a large number of backbench MPs. Approximately 150 MPs now sit on the new committees.

It is also important to remember that the working environment of a committee is different from that of the Chamber. Personal contact during committee sessions is much closer, for only a table (rather than the floor of the House) separates the actors involved. Ideally, a committee's members should work together efficiently, with party beliefs and individual opinions entering the fray only to provide healthy friction. The prevalent belief that select committees are the more rational tools of enquiry, and the Chamber the arena for purely political struggle, should nonetheless not be carried too far. It is party which is still the ever dominant factor in British politics, and party should never be forgotten when discussing select committees.

In sum, the working abilities and powers of select committees remain difficult to pinpoint precisely and the extent of their influence difficult to determine. They merely have the right to call for 'persons, papers and records', and then can only offer 'recommendations'. Their influence does not rely upon sanctions or threats, but upon the expertise and cogency of their reports and upon how far government is willing to initiate, review or change a policy.

Gradual Development

The lengthy controversy surrounding the establishment of select committees might easily lead the uninitiated to suppose that such committees of various types have been widely used in the House for centuries. The Tudor and Stuart Parliaments, for example, made extensive use of committees. But select committees fell into disuse from the mid-Victorian period onwards. The Parliament of the 'Golden Age' of Bagehot conducted only a relatively small amount of business and this could be coped with easily by the Chamber. Only belatedly, during the second half of this century, did the House of Commons and even governments begin to realize that committees would need to be more extensively used in order to cope with the heavier responsibilities of ruling in the age of 'big government'. Unfortunately, governments, who on the whole have enjoyed the crucial prerogative of establishing or abolishing committees, have usually favoured the device of standing committees to secure the quicker passage of their growing legislative programmes without seeking to establish a corresponding balance of select committees to help to oversee this extra activity. The Commons, too, must also share some of the blame for only lately recognizing that it could not rely solely upon the work of the individual MP and the instrument of the Chamber. After decades of complacency, it was not until the mid-1960s, after a campaign by some younger MPs and a group of academics, that any serious attempts were made to institute a more comprehensive band of select committees. Indeed, as late as 1959, in a now infamous judgement, a Select Committee on Procedure refused to recommend the increased use of specialist committees in the House, believing them to be 'a radical constitutional innovation'.[3] That committee was, historically and procedurally, wrong.

For the first half of this century, scrutiny via select committees largely consisted of the Public Accounts Committee, set up by Gladstone, and the Estimates Committee, first established in 1912 by Lloyd George. The PAC, the first of the modern committees, proved an immediate success and remains a senior and prestigious select committee. The Estimates Committee, however, suffered a chequered career, being first directed to 'effect economies' in the administration of the state, and forbidden to question or investigate policy. Lloyd George as Prime Minister felt, in common with most of his successors, that a select committee given the power to question policy would threaten the stability of government. Gradually, however, successive Estimates Committees managed to consider policy within their remit, and after 1945 experiments in sub-dividing the committee implied a serious attempt to specialize in certain areas. But the committee remained largely unpopular with backbenchers, it lacked the prestige of the PAC, and thus occupied only a peripheral political role. Its ability to exert a continuous and vigorous role of scrutiny is questionable, although it could be maintained that the committee was an important stepping stone in the lengthy progress toward the acceptance and establishment of select committees in the House.[4]

Dissatisfaction with the patchy provision of select committees for the House has occasionally boiled over, usually coinciding with a period of criticism of Britain's central institutions, the result of a poor economic or political performance. Thus during the Depression of the 1920s and early 1930s the feasibility of a more rigorous select-committee structure was examined. Parliament was being blamed for the nation's ills, and its ability to function primarily as a 'talking shop' was called into question. The cry went out 'Parliament must be reformed,' and select committees were again advocated by critics intent on improving the image and performance of the institution. Unless the Commons was modernized in this fashion they feared that its legitimacy would suffer, thereby directly threatening the operation of democracy. In a time of crisis, they argued, Parliament had to be seen to be working well. A Committee on Procedure reported that an enlarged Estimates Committee should be established and allowed to comment on policy as well as administrative matters.[5] However, this advice was rejected; the government was more concerned with managing the crisis engendered by the Depression than tinkering with the accountability procedures of Parliament. The government adopted a siege mentality, perhaps understandable in view of the problems they faced, and Neville Chamberlain explained to the House on behalf of the government its suspicions that 'a new Estimates Committee could not deal with major matters of policy without encroaching upon the powers of the Executive.'[6]

This limiting view was to permeate the whole debate over reform for a further 30 years. On the one hand, governments were seeking ever greater powers to push through their expanding legislative programmes ever more quickly, but on the other the Commons was not being allowed to develop correspondingly expert methods of scrutiny. Nor, it must be said, did backbenchers in the House realize that, coupled to party disciplines, the effects of streamlining procedures and of delegating more responsibility to Whitehall were shuttling away their opportunities for critical analysis. This highly unbalanced development was epitomized by a series of reforms in the late 1940s.[7] The Attlee government's reconstruction and welfare programmes required massive amounts of legislation and expenditure. A rapid series of Procedure Reports recommended that, in order to expedite the business of the government, which after all enjoyed a comprehensive mandate, standing committees should be used much more widely than previously. The government readily accepted this proposal, and now most Bills, with certain exceptions, are processed through standing committees. This was an eminently sensible reform, aimed at rationalizing and speeding up the legislative procedure; it is now accepted that the Chamber alone could never deal with all its business without recourse to such committees. But it was also a one-sided reform, since the Attlee government was not prepared to compensate for its increased use of standing committees with an enhanced role for select committees to help scrutinize the extra business that Parliament was now technically obliged to oversee. The tentative use of sub-committees by the Estimates Committee as an experiment in specialization fell far short of subjecting any particular government department to consistent scrutiny.

Throughout the 1950s, with only a small hiccough over Suez in 1956, both Parliament and government seemed content to allow the business of the House to be processed at an increased pace and volume, and congratulated themselves that the traditional methods of scrutiny and accountability could still be adequate. By 1959, with the publication of the Procedure Report mentioned above, the prospects for radical select-committee reform appeared to be at their lowest ebb. The report had even refused to sanction an experimental committee on colonial affairs.

It appeared that Parliament was satisfied with its limited use of the Public Accounts and Estimates Committees. However, as in the 1930s, the 1960s turned out to be a decade of criticism. A new reform movement sprang up, dissatisfied with the overall performance of the Commons.[8] Critics argued that whilst Parliament might still retain, through the doctrine of sovereignty, the ultimate right to topple governments, in everyday terms the average backbencher enjoyed very little political clout. Reformers believed that, without upsetting the delicate arrangements of stable government, backbenchers could be afforded a more influential role if they were prepared to use the instrument of the select committee to question regularly the actions of the executive in a thoroughgoing manner, and by acting collectively produce informative and incisive reports. The divisions caused by party would be blurred in the pursuit of truth. Information, presuming they could extract it from Whitehall, was deemed to be power.

In 1964, the pressures to reform at last led to the division of the Estimates Committee into sub-committees, empowered to specialize in given areas, and in 1966, with Richard Crossman as the new progressive Labour Leader of the House, further 'experimental' reforms were promised. Two new select committees were established, to deal with agriculture and science and technology respectively. Although Crossman had stressed that their work was meant only to be 'a cautious advance in the revival of Parliamentary control over the Executive',[9] the near euphoria which surrounded the announcement of the now famous 'Crossman reforms' seemed to deafen enthusiasts to the tone of caution in his speech; many conveniently forgot that the establishment of these committees would not necessarily entail any diminution in governmental power, but only serve to make the operation of that power more accountable. The more sensible reformers of the period, such as Bernard Crick, struggled to provide a workable formula for future committee development within the existing power structure; others fell into the trap of predicting a new 'Golden Age' just around the corner. In the 1960s the situation remained unclear and far from satisfactory: the later years of the decade were characterized by much chopping and changing of committees and an inefficient degree of overlap between the newer committees and the Estimates Committee. Nevertheless, the reforms of the period, although overestimated in importance, did sow the seeds for further, more wide-reaching reform in the decade to follow.

A further step towards the establishment of a permanent and comprehensive set of select committees followed the publication of yet another Procedure Committee Report in 1969.[10] After the general election in 1970, the Heath Government finally enacted its recommendation to abolish the Estimates Committee and rationalize the committees of the Crossman period by setting up a new and all-embracing Expenditure Committee with six 'functional' sub-committees covering the major areas of governmental activity. The reform attempted to achieve the establishment of an efficient and comprehensive set of specialized subject committees to serve the House, albeit technically under the umbrella of just one.

According to the Procedure Committee, the new committee should have the three-fold task of examining expenditure, the implications of policy objectives, and departmental administration and management. This was a far cry from, for example, the early Estimates Committee which was directed merely to 'effect economies' wherever possible. But even the establishment of the Expenditure Committee soon came to be regarded as a stop-gap reform. Although it had succeeded in rationalizing the hotch-potch created by the 1960s experiments, it lacked, in the words of one leading backbencher, the 'necessary constitution' to undertake a rigorous scrutiny role.[11] Despite the vast improvement which the committee represented in terms of coverage and the examination of policy, the criticism it attracted reflects the higher expectations generated amongst MPs after a decade and a half of experiment. And as Philip Norton has explained in greater depth, the 1970s witnessed a resurrected spirit amongst a significant number of MPs anxious to remind their parties that they could not always be relied upon in the division lobbies, nor indeed during committee voting. This new spirit of dissension coincided with and proved complementary to the calls for a full system of specialized and permanent select committees in the House of Commons.

The 1979 Reforms: 'Thin Ends of Wedges'

In 1975 in the Queen's Speech the Labour government had been obliged to promise a 'major review' of Parliamentary procedure, and in debate a few months later MPs voted to appoint a Select Committee on Procedure to undertake the task. The government was at pains to stress that the committee should not be seeking fundamental changes in the relationship between the executive and the legislature. However, in its First Report, published in July 1978,[12] the committee wasted no time in repudiating this over-cautious approach. For the committee, reform would not prove effective if governments always remained assured of their legislation being passed, condescendingly allocating to backbenchers a 'worthwhile' but essentially marginal role in some obscure committee. The Procedure Committee sought to strike a new balance, giving select committees the remit to investigate the actions of government at *every* stage in the development of policy, not simply to serve as reactive mechanisms to a policy which had been already decided upon.

The committee came out in favour of 'specialist' rather than 'departmental' committees, partly because it was felt they would be able to build upon the work already done by the sub-committees of the Expenditure Committee, and also because the divisions of specialization they were to propose mostly reflected departmental divisions anyway. The proposed set of 14 new committees would each attach themselves to a relevant main 'client' department, but would also be allowed the freedom to range wider in their enquiries if necessary, thus allaying fears of compartmentalization.

In its report, the committee felt that only about 140 MPs would be needed to staff the system they proposed, quelling doubts that past recruitment problems might be exacerbated by an extension in the use of committees. The optimum number of MPs on each committee, usually nine or eleven, would ensure that they acted as 'single, cohesive, investigative units'. The Procedure Report further recommended that the new committees should command greater resources and research facilities, as well as the power to insist upon the attendance of ministers and civil servants, and to call upon the production of any information which they reasonably deemed to be relevant to their enquiries. Hostile confrontation between governments and the new committees would be the least desirable by-product of their proposals. What the Procedure Committee strove for was a *workable* relationship between Westminster and Whitehall, involving greater co-operation on both sides. Committee work was to become an integral part of the Westminster structure, offering a possible career alternative for those MPs who chose to specialize in a particular field. Importantly, the committee recommended that select committees should become permanent, i.e. established for at least the length of a Parliament. Previously they had been sessional.

It is clear from reading the report that expectations of reform ran high. On its publication, the Labour Leader of the House, Michael Foot, a traditionalist opposed to an extension of select-committee operations, attempted to shelve the report, but MPs on both sides of the House demanded a debate on its recommendations, effectively keeping the pot boiling even though the 1979 general election intervened. Despite much opposition from within the new Conservative Cabinet, support for the scheme continued to grow amongst backbenchers, aided by a sympathetic and enthusiastic Leader of the House, Norman St John-Stevas. On 25 June 1979, the House voted in favour of a new committee system by 248 votes to 12. The new committees established are listed in table 3.1. Existing committees which still remained after this major shake-up were the Public Accounts Committee and the Select Committees for the Ombudsman, Delegated Legislation and European Legislation. Altogether, there are now 27 select committees, the remainder dealing with the Commons' internal matters.

As usual, the advocates were ecstatic, the cynics indifferent and the traditionalists hostile. Mr St John-Stevas, as an advocate, claimed that the changes 'could constitute the most important Parliamentary reforms of the century'.[13] It is always sensible to be wary of such sweeping statements, but it is nevertheless important to remember that it was the snowballing pressure of the House which effectively created the new set of committees, not a government cautiously experimenting with a marginal role for backbenchers. George Cunningham, a member of the Procedure Committee, remained more down-to-earth than the Leader of the House, maintaining that their recommendations were not intended to be ultimate solutions to the problems of Parliamentary accountability, but more 'thin ends of wedges', designed to develop from a securely organized base a high level of expertise, permanence and scrutiny. The new committees were expected

Table 3.1 House of Commons' select committees, 1984 (first appointed 1979, reappointed 1983)

Committee	Principal government departments covered	Chairman	Number of members
Agriculture	Ministry of Agriculture, Fisheries and Food	John Spence (Con.)	11[a]
Defence	Ministry of Defence	Sir Humphrey Atkins (Con.)	11
Education, Science and Arts	Department of Education and Science	Sir William van Straubenzee (Con.)	11[a]
Employment	Department of Employment	Ron Leighton (Lab.)	11[a]
Energy	Department of Energy	Ian Lloyd (Con.)	11
Environment	Department of the Environment	Sir Hugh Rossi (Con.)	11
Foreign Affairs	Foreign and Commonwealth Office	Sir Anthony Kershaw (Con.)	11
(Sub-committee[b]		vacant	—)
Home Affairs	Home Office	Sir Edward Gardner (Con.)	11
(Sub-committee[c]		John Wheeler (Con.)	5)
Trade and Industry[c]	Department of Industry, Department of Trade	Kenneth Warren (Con.)	11
Scottish Affairs	Scottish Office	David Lambie (Lab.)	13
Social Services	Department of Health and Social Security	Mrs Renee Short (Lab.)	11[a]
Transport	Department of Transport	Harry Cowans (Lab.)	11
Treasury and Civil Service	Treasury, Management and Personnel Office, Board of Inland Revenue, Board of Customs and Excise	Terence Higgins (Con.)	11
(Sub-committee		Austin Mitchell (Lab.)	5)
Welsh Affairs	Welsh Office	Gareth Wardell (Lab.)	11

[a] 9 members in the 1979–83 Parliament. [b] Not appointed in the new Parliament. [c] Entitled the Industry and Trade Committee in the 1979–83 Parliament.

to build upon an unprecedented level of backbench support for their operations and upon the tacit understanding that governments henceforth must accept the permanent existence and working of such a comprehensive system. If MPs are now prepared to allot a significant proportion of their crowded schedules to more schedules to more committee work, governments too should join enthusiastically in the pursuit of 'good government', which, after all, is the primary aim.

The new select committees were, indeed, parliamentary creations; as a further reinforcement of their 'independence', the Committee of Selection, instead of the whips, was vested with the power to choose committee members, and a Liaison Committee was established, composed of the chairmen of the committees, to help direct the overall development of the system. It would appear that the system as it stands is determined to remain independent of government and even Opposition front-bench interference. Politics, of course, will always play some part, but select committees are now far more the jealous preserve of the backbencher in Parliament.

Activities and Influence

The committees are charged with examining the work and expenditure of government departments, and the effect of government policies, and thence reporting back to the House. The orthodox reaction to a report usually comes in the form of a 'Government Reply' to the points made. Even in this area, departments are being pressed to provide as quick a response as practical so as not to lose the momentum and topicality of the enquiry. Two months was the optimum reply period suggested by the Procedure Committee and generally departments have tried to adhere to this limit, although there have been a number of disappointing exceptions.

But, bearing in mind their powers only to advise and recommend, how effectively do they operate, and what should they be expected to achieve? If we accept Michael Mezey's hypothesis that Parliament, having few powers to initiate legislation, must wait to 'react' to government proposals, then the acid test of the worth of select committees should rest upon their ability to speed up those reactions. If a committee can collect information, if a committee can closely question ministers, civil servants and recognized experts, and if it can produce reports on relevant, ideally topical issues, then it has a chance to contribute to the work of Parliament.

Certainly, in terms of their sheer level of activity, the committees

Table 3.2   Select committees, meetings, 1979-1983

| | Number of meetings | | |
Committee	Evidence sessions	Deliberative sessions	Total
Agriculture	59	40	99
Defence	92	67	159
Education, Science and Arts	106	60	166
Employment	84	28	112
Energy	83	67	150
Environment	47	69	116
Foreign Affairs	71	64	135
(Sub-committee	50	64	114)
Home Affairs	55	53	108
(Sub-committee	65	45	110)
Industry and Trade	72	47	119
Scottish Affairs	67	51	118
Social Services	95	59	154
Transport	89	48	137
Treasury and Civil Service	73	79	152
(Sub-committee	38	36	74)
Welsh Affairs	84	33	117
Totals[a]	1,230	910	2,140

[a]Meetings of sub-committees included in the totals. (Visits made by committees where no evidence was taken and no formal deliberations made are not included.)

Source: Calculated from data in Parliamentary Written Answer, *HC Deb*. 46, cols 645–6.

would appear to be striving to achieve such ends. In the last Parliament, they held more than 2000 meetings (table 3.2). Members were assiduous in their attachment to and attendance at committees: turnover of members was low, attendance at meetings was high (table 3.3). Ministers and civil servants were summoned to appear regularly. In the Parliament a total of 1,312 officials made 1,799 appearances before the committees; 161 ministers also appeared before them. In the Parliament, the committees issued a total of 193 reports. As table 3.4 reveals, the largest number emanating from one committee was 24 – from the Treasury and Civil Service Committee.

The committees, then, can hardly be faulted for their energy. But energy and effectiveness are not synonymous terms. As any good sportsman will testify, reaction also involves anticipation, and usually

Table 3.3   Select committees: attendance and turnover rates, 1979–1983

Committee	Attendance average (%)	Turnover[a] (%)
Agriculture	78	44
Defence	73	36
Education, Science and Arts	69	11
Employment	71	66
Energy	64	36
Environment	69	64
Foreign Affairs	78	64
(Sub-committee	72	67)
Home Affairs	81	55
(Sub-committee	89	60)
Industry and Trade	76	27
Scottish Affairs	78	85
Social Services	71	44
Transport	70	18
Treasury and Civil Service	88	36
(Sub-committee	69	86)
Welsh Affairs	78	27

[a]This figure represents the percentage change in membership based on those who were members of the committee at the beginning of the existence of the Committee and who remained members at the dissolution.

Source: Parliamentary Written Answer, *HC Deb*. 46, col. 633.

serves to provide an extra crucial edge to performance. The whole argument now surrounding the committees hinges not so much on their recognized success in developing an energetic information and scrutiny mechanism, as upon their anticipation of the political issues coming up. Thus, as an extension to their functions, it is hoped that they will become embroiled in the decision-making process from a very early stage, long before any final decisions are taken. There are, of course, a lot of 'ifs' in this formula, but gradually select committees appear to be, in the words of the present Leader of the House, John Biffen, entering 'into the bloodstream' of the political process, despite their amorphous powers.

Christopher Price, chairman of the Education, Science and Arts Select Committee between 1979 and 1983, neatly encapsulated the expectations and problems caused by their remit, when he described his committee's visit to the US Congress, an institution much more

Table 3.4   Select committee reports, 1979–1983

Committee	Number of reports issued
Agriculture	6
Defence	13
Education, Science and Arts	19
Employment	11
Energy	11
Environment	9
Foreign Affairs	21
Home Affairs	20
Industry and Trade	20
Scottish Affairs	8
Social Services	11
Transport	15
Treasury and Civil Service	24
Welsh Affairs	5
Total	193

committee-orientated than the House of Commons:

Which month of the year did we vote on appropriation? Well, never actually – we didn't have any control over the raising of money or the spending of it. Ah, said my Congressman, he understood. The House of Commons was a legislative body; so committee controlled the passage of legislation. Was that a rewarding task? Well, no, I had to say, we had no connection with legislation. . . . Had I thought it worth continuing, I would have explained that the only power we committees had was to send for 'persons and papers'. . . . Curiously these apparently impotent Select Committees have achieved some influence . . . but only when they make themselves more expert than Ministers and Civil Servants. The former isn't too difficult; the latter will take a little more time.[14]

The work of the Education, Science and Arts Committee does, in fact, serve as a good example of a committee using its rather vague remit to scrutinize and influence govenment. During the 1979–83 Parliament the committee examined a very wide range of topics, including higher education, the British Library, the secondary-school curriculum, public and private funding of the arts, biotechnology, school meals and prison education. Over the four years, it also began to hold 'financial' and 'scrutiny' sessions as part of an exercise in monitoring the work and accounts of the Department of Education and Science. It also had cause to complain of the lack of information received from ministers and civil servants, as well as of a poor or late response to certain of its reports. The chairman vigorously strove to adapt the work of his committee to take advantage of current issues. The committee issued a number of short reports, breaking free from the past 'Royal Commission' syndrome which dogged earlier committees and which demanded the production of lengthy and usually late reports, no longer relevant to the political process. If a committee can issue a quick but reasoned comment on a topical subject it achieves greater impact.

In the committee, despite the powerful presence of Mr Price as a Labour chairman, the Conservative majority prevailed in most votes. However, the Conservatives were not afraid to criticize their own government. The committee as a whole spoke out against a number of the Conservative government's policies, for example on the issue of raising the level of overseas students fees and the expenditure cuts in higher education. They produced several reports describing particular policies as 'hasty', 'ill-conceived' or 'wrong'. Although the committee could not claim to have reversed the executive's education policies, it was instrumental in helping to pressurize the government on various issues, and acted as an access point for all the groups concerned with education-policy decisions to enable them to make their views known to the decision-takers. The committee was an important voice in the successful campaign to allocate more money to foreign students to study in this country, and one of the first to recommend the establishment of the National Advisory Board for the higher education sector.

The experiences of the committee also show that ministers and civil servants must now be prepared to be as helpful as possible during their evidence-giving sessions. Mark Carlisle, the then Secretary of State for Education, consistently fell foul of the committee for refusing to be as co-operative as they would have liked, failing to divulge information which he deemed to be safeguarded by the conventions of ministerial responsibility. The committee, particularly their chairman, were not impressed and his political reputation appeared to suffer as a result of his negative performance.

Led by a chairman fired by a crusade against the 'corridors of power' the committee was often at odds with the executive, for members made it plain they would not tolerate covering-up tactics or a slow reply. Government departments usually do their best to be helpful, although until some formula is worked out, perhaps involving a Freedom of Information Act, the provision of the facts to select committees will always be a sticky point. In his assessment of the committee's first two years at work, Mr Price reported to the Liaison Committee that the more flexible working methods they had adopted (through varying the levels and sizes of enquiries as well as through their use of 'financial' and 'scrutiny' sessions) meant that they could react to current concerns that much more quickly. He went on: 'we have been able to respond to Government initiatives on a continuing basis, and create an opportunity for the scrutiny of Government policy *as it develops*.'[15]

The influence of the Education Committee was neatly summarized by Mr Price in his report to the Liaison Committee:

Our British Library report was immediately followed by a government decision to build it, our higher education report led to the establishment of a National Advisory Board in the public sector, our 'Proms' report restored the concerts to the Albert Hall and our ICCROM report re-established the British subscription to that organisation.[16]

Other committees have been able to make comparable claims. The Energy Committee, for example, 'achieved perceptible shifts in Government policy, e.g. the scaling down of the nuclear power commitment and a transfer of the emphasis to economic rather than environmental considerations';[17] it also persuaded the government to revise its fiscal regime in North Sea oil-depletion policy.[18] The Foreign Affairs Committee influenced both the British and Canadian governments in debates on the repatriation of the Canadian constitution; indeed, it 'persuaded the Canadian Government to accept some of its thoughts about how the Canadian Prime Minister might accommodate the Canadian provinces regarding that legislation'.[19] The Employment Committee persuaded the Manpower Services Commission to include the long-term unemployed as one of its priorities ('It was an important policy shift which Jim Callaghan had not managed when ... in Government').[20] The Home Affairs Committee influenced the restructuring of procedures for dealing with complaints against the police and, the best-known example, it persuaded the government to repeal the so-called 'sus' laws. These are examples of select-committee influence, in some instances significant influence, upon Government policy, influence that would not have been achieved had the committees not existed.

Christopher Price lost his seat in the 1983 general election. Writing subsequently in *The House Magazine*, he offered these observations to potential select-committee members: 'Working on a Select Committee can be a hugely creative parliamentary experience and one from which it is possible to influence long-term policy very much more directly than from the Whips Office or junior Ministerial office. I recommend it with enthusiasm.'[21]

Conclusion

Select committees have come a long way since the early, somewhat unsuccessful days of the old Estimates Committee. Their structure is now reasonably permanent and most importantly retains a momentum geared towards further improvement. The odds are, however, against yet more procedural change. In line with one of the Procedure Committee's recommendations, the House has experimented with special standing committees which allow a standing committee to examine witnesses for a short time as if it were a select committee (see appendix 1). The ultimate and extreme outcome of this experiment would be the abolition of standing committees as we know them and the employment of select committees to oversee the work of their client departments, *including* legislation. When this point is reached (and the House is a long way from it yet), the arguments over their functions will become even more complicated.

The improvement has been noticeable. Select committees might complain that their powers are not great enough or that they are still not assured of a debate in the House, but few would doubt that their work has generally improved the standard of work and understanding in the House. Service on a select committee is beneficial to an individual MP, and committee reports help the work of the whole House.

Samuel Johnson once had occasion to remind a certain lady of his acquaintance, 'Expectations improperly indulged must end in disappointment,' and it is always best not to exaggerate the powers of select committees. Old lags of the House examine the latest set of committees and see nothing new; indeed, in the best traditions of Westminster nothing *startling* has happened. But it would also be wrong not to recognize the very real effect they have had on the working MPs, ministers and civil servants – select committees have entered, as John Biffen said, into the 'bloodstream' of British politics. They have not changed the working relationship of Parliament and the executive, but they have at least improved it.

Notes

1 The Osthmotherly Memorandum, drawn up by an assistant secretary in the Civil Service Department, outlines for civil servants the issues or areas which they should not be drawn upon: civil service advice to ministers; questions in the field of public controversy; the level at which decisions are taken; and inter-departmental discussions.

2 D. Judge, *Backbench Specialisation in the House of Commons* (London: Heinemann, 1981).

3 Select Committee on Procedure 1958/9, HC 92.

4 See N. Johnson, *Parliament and Administration* (London: George Allen & Unwin, 1966).

5 HC 161 (1931).

6 *HC Deb.* 277, cols 669–70.

7 See HC 144 (1946/7), HC 98 (1947/8), HC 202 (1947/8), HC 283 (1948/9), HC 131 (1950).

8 See, for example, B. Crick, *The Reform of Parliament*, 2nd edn (London: Weidenfeld & Nicolson, 1970).

9 *HC Deb.* 738, col. 494.

10 HC 401 (1968/9).

11 E. du Cann, 'Reflections on the Control of Public Expenditure in the U.K.', *The Parliamentarian*, 57(3), July 1976.

12 HC 588 (1977/8).

13 *HC Deb.* 969, cols 33–252.

14 *New Statesman*, 11 June 1982.

15 *Report to the Liaison Committee*, HC 92 (1982/3).

16 Ibid., p. 48.

17 Ibid., p. 64.

18 I. Lloyd MP, in D. Englefield (ed.), *Commons Select Committees: Catalysts for Progress?* (London: Longman, 1984), p. 71.

19 C. Morris, in Englefield, *Commons Select Committees*, p. 42.

20 J. Golding MP in Englefield, *Commons Select Committees*, p. 70.

21 Quoted in Englefield, *Commons Select Committees*, p. xxv.

4

Representational Changes
The Constituency MP

James W. Marsh

The amount of time and effort devoted to constituency casework by Members of Parliament is one of the few areas of parliamentary life that has changed substantially this century. The importance attached to constituency grievance work has changed dramatically in the past 20 years and MPs and academics alike now accept that one cannot adequately explain or understand the representative function of an MP if one ignores this welfare-officer role. Until the 1960s a 'constituency member' was seen as a failed frontbencher or as someone who had entered Parliament too late to hope for a ministerial position. This view was reflected in academic literature, which concentrated on Members' legislative activities. A casual glance at an MP's timetable today reveals a different set of priorities to that previously presumed to exist and shows that a significant proportion of the backbencher's time is spent carrying out the major role of welfare-rights officer and social worker.

The change in the attitude to, and scope of, constituency casework came in the 1960s with the growth of 'community politics', which meant that local issues and problems were exploited by local parties, at that time usually the Liberal Party, to undermine the sitting MP. Today, it is seen by the incumbent MP and the challengers as an uncontroversial means of securing a reliable base of local support. There is greater importance attached to the potential electoral bonus, especially in marginal seats, where MPs and local parties fight to minimize any bad effects of the usually all-embracing national swing. For example, in the general election of 1979 the Labour Party kept down the swing against it in the marginal seats where MPs took a more aggressive approach to their constituency work.[1] As the election approached, Members of Parliament positively sought grievances, gained higher approval ratings from their constituents, and achieved some success in dissociating themselves where necessary from their national party label. This is a continuous process, and as more MPs see the potential of constituency work they will make greater efforts, increase casework and maintain their demands for staff and services to cope with the new workload. Such speculations were confirmed by the Nuffield General Election Study of May 1979 in an analysis of the lower swing against Labour MPs in marginal constituencies.[2] It was confirmed that a major reason for the low swing in the marginals was the effect of the change in support for the incumbent MP since 1974. The incumbent commands a personal vote, consisting of those who support him as an individual rather than as a national party representative. This personal vote disappears if the MP is defeated. The process continues as the new winner works to build up a personal vote by the next election. For the period 1974 to 1979, it would appear that the personal vote amounted to around 1,500 votes in an average-sized constituency, a figure which may be decisive in a closely contested seat. Whilst one need not doubt the generally admirable motives of MPs doing their casework, here is a realistic assessment of the potential value of such work to a number of MPs.

The changed attitude to constituency casework is evident amongst the MPs and their constituency parties, and in the constituency at large. Increasingly MPs are more willing to expand the scope of their casework activities, resulting in bigger caseloads and rising expectations in both the constituency party and the electoral constituency. MPs today can rarely choose the level of the work they wish to undertake, often as a result of the expectations created by the previous incumbent. It is rapidly becoming evident that the backbench MP may even be approaching a position of 'overload,' as his casework increases even as he maintains his 'amateur' status.

We will see that the time spent by Members of Parliament on such work alone makes it worthy of notice, occupying an estimated two to three hours per day and most of an MP's weekend. Studies of casework have emphasized the importance of the linking of Parliament and its constituencies, and its legitimizing and consent-mobilizing functions. It is in constituency grievance work that the MP performs the function of 'specific representation',[3] and acts as an intermediary between people and the executive – as a transmission belt from the public to the government and vice versa. The MP is the intermediary not only between the citizen and central government but between the citizen and all aspects of public administration. In addition, studying an MP's casework gives a more complete picture of the constituents' perceived relationship with their Member of Parliament.

As we shall see, after contact with the Member of Parliament the constituent is more likely to believe that the MP is doing a good job, a fact which breeds content within the political system.[4] Here the MP is contributing to the stability of the system and controlling the executive and administration in a very practical sense. Thus although constituents vote on the basis of their national party affiliations, they expect their MPs, regardless of party, to protect local interests and attend to constituency work. This work generates high levels of constituency satisfaction and favourable attitudes to MPs, even if there is simultaneous hostility to their party groups or to other parliamentary activity.[5]

The great variety of issues raised with MPs by their constituents demonstrates the inefficacy of the alternative grievance machinery available. It reveals the lack of a comprehensive or co-ordinated complaints system, or perhaps the existence of a system in which the procedures offered are so ineffective, expensive or intimidating that the constituent may feel that the odds are too greatly stacked against him. We might ask why citizens feel the need to approach an MP rather than make use of the alternatives; in answering that question we may discover what the faults are in those alternatives, and perhaps go some way towards remedying them. Ignorance of the alternatives available is not always the reason; indeed the choice of an MP is often based on detailed knowledge of the alternatives. However, where the choice is based on ignorance it illuminates the symbolic aspects of an MP's work: the British citizen may approach his representative about any subject or grievance, a direct appeal against bureaucracy in whatever form.[6]

We will see that constituency grievance work is often a significant source of information for an MP, and a major spur to changes in the law – the means whereby MPs see the fruits of their legislative labours or those of the government. It is here that they can see if the legislation or administrative directives are having the desired effects.

Thus the constituency work of local MPs is a much neglected subject. Understanding the nature of the work, how it is handled by the MP, and all the consequences that flow from it, will ultimately provide a more balanced view of the public status of the modern MP.

The Character of Constituency Casework

What does casework involve, and how is it conducted? Most cases reach the Member of Parliament in two ways. Firstly there is the MP's 'surgery'. As its name suggests this is similar to the traditional doctors' surgery, where patients go along on a particular day and time to obtain treatment and advice. The MP usually establishes a regular place and time in a local hall, room or party office. This is advertised throughout the constituency in the local press, through party publicity and in local libraries. Constituents then come to the surgery and wait to see their MP on any one (or more) of a massive variety of issues and problems.

The other most popular method of contacting the Member of Parliament is to write to the House of Commons; more rarely, the constituent will write to the MP's local party or home address. The MP will handle the case on the basis of this letter or, if it is necessary to have more information, the constituent may be asked to come along to the surgery at the earliest possible date.

The types of case taken to the surgery, or outlined in a letter, are broadly similar, although it has been established that surgery attenders are those less happy with letter-writing. Surgery cases are almost exclusively devoted to problems and are attended more by working-class families. Letter-writers have been judged to be more likely to be middle class, with a greater tendency to express wider political views as they air their problems.

The single greatest problem brought to the attention of any MP is that of housing. This can amount to over 50 per cent of all the cases that may be received. Such cases present the MP with a range of problems. Housing is a local authority matter which has no direct administrative link with the MP. It simply remains for the MP to take up cases on the basis of superior knowledge and experience, and to help the constituent to get as much satisfaction as possible within the limits of the particular case. Most MPs seem aware that given the real limits of housing stock, and given the fact that another unfortunate family may be waiting for that same transfer, they must not bully the local authority into a partial decision. It is simply a question of stating the constituent's case in the best possible way and bringing all the relevant details to the attention of the local authority. For instance a family may have applied for a move to a particular new housing estate for a number of years. In their frustration they contact their MP who takes up their case. On closer examination the MP discovers that one of the young children in the family is suffering from asthma. When this is brought to the attention of the local authority's medical officer the family's grading and place on the waiting list is changed, giving them a much greater chance of a move.

Other major problem areas involve such problems as pensions and social services. Depending on the character of the constituency, the MP may receive problems involving planning applications, educational placements, grants or income tax – quite simply, the range of problems resulting from constituents' contacts with local or central government, where the constituent is dissatisfied, confused or demands more information. Amongst this mass of broadly similar cases there is the occasional individual test case, a case where the MP feels that the constituent has been badly treated or may be the innocent victim of an anomaly in the law. This is normally pursued to the end in a blaze of local publicity. Added to this is the human-interest case where the remedy may be beyond governmental responsibility but where the Member may launch a campaign to help a constituent. One such case concerned a mother whose son was killed in action in Aden. It is the Army's policy to bury their dead where they have fallen, so the family were unable to have the body brought home. In response to the MP's appeals, enough money was raised to send the family to visit the grave. The result was not satisfactory to all but went a long way to easing a mother's loss.

For any one case an MP usually writes between three and five letters. In some the time in letter-writing alone could take hours, in addition to visits and deputations. However, in most cases the MP will acknowledge to the constituent that the case will be pursued. Contact is made with the relevant authorities and this information is passed back to the constituent. The MP is the middle man, the advice bureau, amateur lawyer or housing officer; the person who takes up the case because there may be no one else willing to do so, someone who is able to command instant respect and attention from national and local government officials.

Constituency Work as a Source of Information

The number of constituents who have at some stage contacted their MP is usually put at about 8 to 10 per cent of a constituency. Any opinion or market research agency would be very satisfied with such a figure as a basis for making an accurate assessment of the concerns of any group. This 'sample' is even more accurate with regard to this aspect of an MP's work, namely the redress of individual grievances. It may be accepted that many of the political views expressed to MPs by constituents are not those of the 'silent majority', but this is not the main purpose of the information. The MP is used as a 'court of appeal' or ombudsman, a function confirmed by many studies of correspondence to MPs from constituents.[7] Those who seek help from their MP in the greatest numbers are those wanting help or advice in cases of maladministration or general personal difficulties. Consequently the 8 to 10 per cent of constituents who make contact with their MP are an excellent source of information. They represent most closely that group which suffers most from bad or impersonal administration. The contact figures are high if one presumes that maladministration surely does not affect more than a minority of the individuals in any constituency. Such people only contact their MP when adversely affected by administrative actions. Higher contact figures would reveal a breakdown in accepted standards of fairness and efficiency in public administration.

Contact with constituents thus represents a major source of information about the effects of national and local government actions. This was confirmed by Dowse in his survey of MPs in 1963:[8] 65.6 per cent of Labour MPs and 58.6 per cent of Conservative MPs thought that their surgeries helped them get 'a feel' of the electorate. Information so gained makes a substantial contribution to the general flow of information that an MP receives, and reveals 'the real preoccupations of the ordinary elector'.[9] Alan Beith MP has commented that if it were not for such knowledge MPs would have little idea of what was politically important to pursue at any one time.[10] Not everyone would agree with such a view since the typicality of many of the complainants is open to challenge, but without doubt casework provides information about the effects of legislation and about those anomalies and injustices resulting from badly thought out or poorly constructed legislation. The information allows the MP to pursue campaigns and launch attacks on actual or proposed government legislation. Each Member of Parliament has his or her own special interests and pursuits, often derived from previous constituency cases.

MPs use constituency cases in a number of ways. Mostly they draw wider significance from an individual case, or cite cases as concrete examples of the adverse effects of governmental or administrative decisions. The significance of these real examples should not be underestimated, for as Alan Beith notes, 'The deficiency which shows itself up in a statistical form is likely to wait until it appears in the personal form of a constituent.'[11]

This contact and personal knowledge gives the constituency MP a moral right to pursue justice in debates and at Question Time; the right to press government ministers on behalf of an individual or group of whom the ministers may be unaware, or on behalf of those who may have special circumstances that have not been considered. Each individual case gives to the MP the right to a degree of impatience in his enquiries. All this would be lost if the constituency link was broken, as would occur under some systems of proportional representation. Under a party-list system of proportional representation, constituency-elected MPs might clash with listed MPs. The constituency MPs could claim first-hand knowledge and accuse the listed MPs of being out of touch. It would be a hard accusation to repudiate.

Constituency Work and Job Satisfaction

A major benefit derived from constituency casework is the enormous satisfaction that it gives to the majority of MPs. Barker and Rush, in their study of constituency work, discovered that 'Nearly 40 per cent of our 109 respondents felt that the time spent on their post was the most valuable part of their work as MPs . . . while the role of the MP as a Welfare Officer was welcomed or accepted by 60 per cent.'[12] Any MP can decide to concentrate on casework. No invitation is needed from the government. It simply requires a commitment from the MP to devote the necessary time and effort. This is of particular comfort to those MPs not chosen, or who have no desire, to serve in government.

In the past not being selected for government relegated the MP to the ranks of the typical 'constituency MP'. This 'constituency man' was more likely to be Labour, older, have fewer outside commitments, or have won election unexpectedly. He was often described as uninspiring and middle-aged, and was likely to have had previous experience on a local council. This is no longer the pattern. MPs are now willing to spend greater time on casework (and less time on their traditional legislative functions), expanding its scope to include local government problems and the whole range of maladministration.

MPs receive great public approval through such work, whilst getting great satisfaction from their successes in the face of the frustrations of Parliamentary life. Indeed this increased amount of time and constituency work may be a reflection of the growth of those frustrations. The average MP plays a very small part in the formation of policy, often managing only the occasional intervention in debates in a mostly empty chamber. Casework provides an area of work where the MP can feel that he is having a significant impact and exerting some degree of influence, heightening the morale of the MP and giving great job satisfaction.[13] Within limits the MP can choose the level of work, but there are now unavoidable demands made on MPs as administrative experts: the state plays an increasing part in the lives of individuals and the administration of the services of the welfare state becomes increasingly complex. Thus whether by choice or not, the amount of casework undertaken by MPs has increased considerably. As long ago as 1967, only 6 per cent of Labour MPs and 11 per cent of Conservative MPs did not hold constituency surgeries.[14]

To get a detailed estimation of the workload it is useful to look at letter counts between the MP and constituents. This can be an accurate estimate of the workload because between 60 and 85 per cent of contacts involve correspondence alone.[15] The findings of Barker and Rush, that 75 per cent of MPs received 25 to 74 letters per week, and that 90 per cent received 25 to 100 letters per week, covers most of the studies of constituency casework.[16] In addition to this sizeable quantity of constituency mail there is the mail from outside the constituency which is often directed at the more prominent Members of the House.

A more detailed and interesting study of an MP's postbag is that of Morrell, with a close examination of the letter-flow between the MP, constituents and other agencies. The Member in question, Tony Benn, received an average of 24 letters per week from constituents, with an average of 17 per week from agencies in response to letters written by the MP on behalf of his constituents. He sent out a further 37 letters per week to constituents, and an average of 17 per week on behalf of his constituents. In total in one year (1972–3) he sent out 5,011 letters. Mr Benn has estimated that he contacted some 35,000 people in the course of his duties as a constituency MP in Bristol.

If these letter-counts and cases are converted into hours, it appears that an MP must spend two to three hours per day on casework, and probably most of the weekend. One must also remember that this aspect of the role of an MP does not end during the parliamentary recess. In many cases it probably increases, because certain kinds of cases are 'seasonal', such as complaints concerning the placement of children in local schools or such as the great number of income tax cases that an MP handles.

The large variation in the quantity of work done by Members is dependent on a number of factors. The most frequent are connected with the size and character of the constituency. This will determine the number of constituents to be served and the type of problem most likely to occur. Thus inner-city constituents will present their Member with a large number of cases, mostly concerned with housing and social security problems. Whether the constituency is a rural or urban seat will mean a difference in workload, as will the number of young or old and retired individuals in any one area. These are the groups most frequently in need of the social services and therefore most frequently in contact with administrators of the services. The attitude of the MP to the work is also a crucial variable, as this is an area of work where the Member can do much to stimulate demand. The availability of other grievance agencies will cause variations in the numbers received but it is not simply a case of the other agencies acting as sieves, because some agencies, such as Citizens' Advice Bureaux, actually refer cases to their Member of Parliament. The distance from London and the marginality of the seat are also of significance, although there is contradictory evidence on these points. One MP had no doubt as to the significance of marginality: 'it depends on your political position within your constituency party, the ability and inclinations of your local councillors and whether the seat is marginal. Some MPs have no alternative but to take everything that comes their way.'[17]

Constituency Work and the Demands of Constituents

Constituents clearly want their MP to protect the constituency, to put local interests first, and most definitely to be available for help at all times (table 4.1).[18]

Table 4.1   What do constituents expect their MPs to do?

Role	%
Ombudsman	19
Protecting constituency	26
Oversight	5
Information	24
Lawmaking (debating and voting)	11
All equal	10

In evaluating the functions of MPs, favourable references are made to the personal qualities of the incumbent, to his or her various qualifications, and to his or her constituency work.[19] So it seems that whilst MPs are so often concerned about the loss of their powers and opportunities for action in the Chamber, their constituents merely want 'a county councillor at Westminster'.[20] Constituents want their MPs to be available to them for help, and after contact with them are more inclined to feel that they are doing a good job. This individual popularity is even more widespread when one considers the 'ripple effect' of the MP's actions. He is rarely helping an individual, more usually it is a whole household, and on occasion whole communities. The public want a middle-man between the ordinary citizen and the remote world of national politics; someone to represent their views at Westminster, and perhaps to convey Westminster's arguments to the constituency. As a consequence of this the most frequent complaint by constituents appears to be the non-availability of the Member, 'and the further away the local Member is from the constituency, taking an outside job, hobnobbing around, the less the public approve.'[21]

The great goodwill produced by casework, and the resulting high expectations for help, cannot simply be the result of the number of changed decisions that the MP can facilitate. Most MPs are justifiably proud of the number of decisions that they do manage to turn in the constituents' favour, but the number of such changed decisions does not correspond with the increased ratings and electoral support. This is clear from the case studies.[22] Munroe's study included a very broad definition of success, but still achieved a changed decision in less than half the cases considered. Success, in the view of constituents, is thus not simply a changed decision in their favour. Most are pleased simply with the efforts made on their behalf by their MP. This will vary with the constituent's expectations, but satisfaction seems to be based on a reassurance that all avenues have been exhausted or that their fears of prejudicial treatment have been allayed. Information on the detailed consideration of their case is of greatest value. Alan Beith feels that very often a reply is all that is required, which overcomes the frustration of the lack of response to any previous enquiries or of the curt replies that administrative agencies regrettably consider adequate.[23] This is when the MP is of the greatest value, securing quick and thorough consideration of constituents' cases. Thus even though much of the MP's constituency work is considered merely as an exercise in forwarding mail, this should now be considered part of a most valuable service, a service most influential in a constituent's evaluation of his MP.

The MP's Relations with the Constituency Party

A reputation as a good constituency MP can be very useful in relations with the constituency party. A store of personal credit gained through constituency work will be very useful in any conflict with the local party. Conversely any lack of commitment to the work may result in problems. A good reputation can soften disagreements and bolster morale at all levels in the constituency party.[24] In a survey of constituency-party activists it was found that 82 per cent felt that casework helped morale and strengthened the local party, whilst 53 per cent believed it improved relations with local party activists. Both factors are particularly important and evident at election time. A further 4 per cent felt that it softened policy disagreements and improved the MP's personal rating in the local party. These figures were reflected in the local activists' views of the functions of an MP, views which closely matched those of the wider public. Accordingly MPs were expected primarily to protect constituency interests. Secondly they were expected to 'help people', and thirdly to 'keep in touch'. Once again the least important functions were the traditional ones of debating, voting and scrutiny of government. Not surprisingly in the light of these results, constituency parties now encourage their MPs to take a greater interest in local affairs and are now more likely to put pressure on the Member to live in or close to the constituency.[25] As we have already seen, until recently the potential electoral advantage from casework was thought to be minimal. The derisive number of votes gained would not decide the fate of a seat and would certainly be a poor return for a great deal of extra work. Consequently the chief motivation to take on work was the MP's own sense of community service and duty. It was simply a part of the job and could not be seen as an effective means of gaining electoral support. Now we know that one of the most effective methods of gaining a local vote and 'familiarity' is through casework – an important consideration when one considers the low swing that may decide the fate of a marginal seat.[26] Before this realization, many MPs reassured us that their motivations were purely altruistic, whilst going through frenzied 'digging in' activities, attending every local function and chasing grievances. Now many are aware of the electoral potential of the work and have stepped up their involvement in the constituency.

The Failure of Other Grievance Agencies

The Member of Parliament has no real place in the official administrative structure. It is relatively easy to justify his or her involvement on behalf of constituents in national government cases, but much harder to do so in respect of local government cases. Nonetheless, it is this latter area where an MP can achieve the greatest success. Not surprisingly, as the scope of local government services has expanded, so the need for a place for individuals to take their complaints has grown. The obvious place to start would seem to be the local councillors, but generally this is not done. Most individuals choose to use the services of their Member of Parliament, for a variety of reasons. Obviously there is the constituents' ignorance of the boundaries of political responsibility: they may not realize that the responsibility for certain services lies with the local government and local representatives. Also, many individuals misunderstand the relationship between central and local government and hope that central government representatives can order local government administrators to comply with their wishes. However, some go to their MP after getting no satisfaction in their grievance from their local councillor; here they are going to the MP as a final court of appeal. In some cases a constituent goes to the MP when in dispute with a councillor.

It must be admitted that MPs are generally better known than local councillors, and are contacted simply on the basis of this greater visibility to the shared constituents. However, most individuals have very little contact with local representatives. They are more likely to have contacts with local officials who administer the services. In addition it does seem that MPs make greater efforts in their casework than councillors. In the past councillors have not really bothered to be available to their constituents, creating a gap that the MP has been obliged to fill. This is not to say that they did not handle the cases that were brought to them or referred to them by the MP, but few went to the extent of grievance chasing.[27] Rees and Smith saw this as a result of the different conception of their sphere of responsibility: 'the work of a councillor is mainly centred on the running of the local administration, and ... he is very much less concerned with acting as an intermediary between electors and the Town Hall departments.'[28]

As a result of all these factors councillors have traditionally spent less time on casework than Members of Parliament. Exactly how much time is spent by each councillor varies with the notoriety, availability, commitment and calibre of the individual councillor, but the Maud Committee noted that on average they spent only 14 per cent of their time on constituency casework.[29] In terms of hours worked this meant that councillors spent an average of 8.4 hours per week on casework, compared with MPs who claimed up to 25 hours per week, with an average of 10 hours.

There is more recent evidence of a new attitude amongst councillors towards their casework, with their greater emphasis on community politics. In a study of the job of local councillor, Heclo found many of the attitudes to the work that we have already noted from the public and MPs.[30] He notes that only 14 per cent of the councillors interviewed gained satisfaction from the more formal aspects of their policy-making role, 'the great satisfaction which the majority of councillors reported is in helping their constituents, not by formal deliberations, but on a fairly direct and personal basis.'[31] As a result of this new attitude Heclo reports higher levels of constituency work, and more regular advice bureaux.

In a survey of councillors in the London Borough of Lambeth in September 1984, there were clear signs that councillors can now rival MPs in their commitment to casework. Thirty-two of the 34 Labour councillors held surgeries once a week, whilst 18 of the 27 Conservative councillors did so. Six of the Labour councillors held surgeries twice a week, whilst all the Labour councillors were available as a group on a further two occasions during the week, amounting to a further three hours' availability. As a whole, all the councillors of Lambeth held a surgery at least once a month, and were willing to take up any cases referred to them.

Despite the new attitude by councillors, MPs are still the more active of the two representatives – in fact and, more significantly, in the minds of constituents, who still are more inclined to go to the MPs. This may be to some 'the tragedy of local government',[32] but it is an instance of the MP doing valuable work from a unique position. MPs are willing to handle both national and local cases, and using their access to higher officials and their capacity to gain greater publicity on any case they may be proving their constituents correct in their decision to complain to their MP rather than to their local councillors.

Obviously more should be done by councillors, but those who do not fear the loss of the constituency-linked MP, such as many electoral reformers, cannot ignore those problems that constituents cannot or will not take to their councillor. No other individual can combine the MP's concern with an understanding of legal and governmental processes. As David Alton notes, the MP satisfies a large number of requirements: 'There are no other bodies, not even such agencies as Citizens' Advice Bureau, which combine moral and sometimes perceived electoral onus to respond with the expertise of an MP, his contacts in higher places [and] the general enthusiasm for helping people.'[33]

The Casework and the MP's Relations within the Constituency

An important by-product of constituency casework is the links that it
fosters with other representatives and administrative bodies in the
area. The principal relationships are those between the MP and locally
elected representatives and between the MP and the local authority
administrative agencies. The relationship between the MP and the
local representative is not the result of any institutional arrangements.
The basis of the contact is simply the responsibility to the people they
serve. The need for the contact between the MP and councillors is the
result of the 50 to 60 per cent of the MP's casework that involves local
authority matters. MPs are increasingly willing to consider local
authority matters and now occupy 'an ambiguous position between
national and local affairs'.[34] This is inevitable if the MP intends fully to
develop the potential of constituency work. Munroe's survey of the
Stoke-on-Trent City Council, just before local government reorganiz-
ation in 1974, found that 85.5 per cent of the council claimed contact
with the city MP in the previous 12 months; 80.8 per cent of such
contact involved constituency casework.[35]

Part of the MP-to-councillor relationship is conducted on party
political lines. Consequently the MP of one party is far more inclined
to use the responsible councillor if that councillor is of the same
political party. This is especially true of Labour MPs[36] who may feel
that the representatives of other parties do not have the same
commitment to constituency work, or perhaps feel that they do not
wish to pass on a possible voter to the opposition. Even without party
political complications there is often a state of tension between MPs
and councillors. This tension results from the role imposed on MPs by
constituents, who demand that the MP acts as an intermediary or
adjudicator between themselves and the local authority. Councillors
feel that on occasion MPs are overstepping their responsibilities, whilst
MPs believe that a large percentage of the work would not reach them
if more councillors took an interest in cases that are strictly local
government matters. However, there is evidence that tension eases
after regular contact as both MPs and councillors realize the mutual
benefits resulting from constituency work.[37]

Perhaps as a result of this state of tension most MPs seem happier
dealing, not with local representatives, but with the local council
officials. Their greater contact with the local officials rather than
representatives puts the MP in the same position as the majority of the

general public. The Bonner study revealed that 60 out of 122 respondents remembered a visit by a local authority worker, other than a rent collector, whilst three-quarters of them remembered visiting the municipal buildings at some time. In comparison only 7 of 122 respondents had experienced personal contact with their councillor.[38] Consequently the MP tries to develop a working relationship with council officials, the individuals who first consider constituents' grievances and administer their services. A working relationship is comparatively easy when the MP merely requests an explanation to pass on to the constituents as reassurance of their fair treatment. Here the relationship is co-operative and open. Difficulties arise when the MP may feel the need to threaten the officials with adverse publicity or parliamentary action to secure their co-operation. Here the MP is taking sides, usually when he feels genuinely that the individual has a case or that the council needs to give greater attention to a constituent's particular circumstances. Inevitably, the MP must attempt some kind of balance between the co-operative ally and the threatening parliamentarian. In most cases, co-operation is achieved.

The Treatment of Central Government Grievances

When faced with a grievance where responsibility rests with central government, an MP has two basic alternatives. He can write discreet letters to ministers or relevant parties, or he can go straight to the established parliamentary procedures to obtain satisfaction. The alternative is real, as there are no compulsory methods for MPs to follow, and to a large degree they are allowed to use the means they choose.[39] However, most MPs do not see the means as alternatives; they regard them as occupying specific places in an escalating scale of redress machinery. For reasons of convenience and likely success, some means are exhausted before others. Specifically their choice is between sending a letter to a minister or using the Parliamentary Commissioner for Administration. Technically the word 'means' is appropriate, as letters to ministers are not procedures of the House, although they are treated by Departments in a specified manner. Parliamentary questions, adjournment debates and the use of the Parliamentary Commissioner are subject to detailed parliamentary procedures.

The escalating scale, as defined by MPs, is based on practical experience of how effective each stage will be. Gregory and Alexander attempted to place the Parliamentary Commissioner in the accepted scale of complaints procedures, and thereby gave an indication of the frequency of the means used, and perhaps less reliably an estimation by MPs of their effectiveness (table 4.2).[40]

Despite vagueness in such responses as 'rarely' and 'often,' the figures do give a basic scale. All MPs write to ministers 'often, very often, always', and more than 90 per cent use the Parliamentary Commissioner 'rarely, very rarely, never'. Here we have the two ends of the scale. The remaining categories are thus options used by MPs to varying degrees. The option of 'talking to a minister' is fairly evenly divided amongst MPs, with 53.4 per cent using the device 'rarely, very rarely, never', and 46.6 per cent using it 'often, very often, always'. This is thus a frequently used option, evenly divided amongst MPs. 'Approaching an official' is the second highest category of 'always', although still low at 7.6 per cent. Overall 54 per cent use it 'often, very often, always', and 45 per cent use it 'very rarely, rarely, never'. Again this is an option fairly evenly divided amongst MPs, with a bias towards use. Using parliamentary questions is the exception rather than the rule, with 64.3 per cent using them 'very rarely, rarely, never', and 35.7 per cent using them 'often, very often'. There were no Members who used them 'always'. Thus this is not a routine procedure and is used when the alternatives fail. A typical constituency case would not result in a parliamentary question. The means with the highest frequency levels are non-parliamentary: firstly a letter to a minister, then approaching a minister or an official. Distinctly behind these come the parliamentary procedures of questions, debates and, most rarely, the Parliamentary Commissioner. In general the ratings of 'effectiveness' match the frequency levels, although the parliamentary techniques, such as parliamentary questions and adjournment debates, score higher than one would have expected. MPs in many cases see their 'effectiveness' in the threat of use, not in the actual use, of such techniques. Therefore many MPs judge the 'effectiveness' of these parliamentary actions by how well they support their previous efforts, fully aware of the interdependency of an MP's weapons in any constituency case.

Frequency may not simply result from actual or perceived effectiveness. A major consideration would be finding time to deal with constituency work amongst other demands. This leaves the MP likely to select the method that proves the most cost-effective in terms of time. We can assume that given the choice MPs will use the method that consumes the least amount of time and work in the face of the huge quantity of constituency mail that Members now receive. Our

Table 4.2 Comparative frequency of use of techniques for seeking the redress of grievances

Frequency	Parliamentary Commissioner	Parliamentary question	Approach official	Talk to minister	Letter to minister
Never	10.9	4.3	18.2	0.7	–
Very rarely/ rarely	80.8	60.0	27.3	52.7	–
Often/very often	8.3	35.7	46.9	45.9	67.5
Always	–	–	7.6	0.7	32.5

scale confirms this view, most MPs merely forwarding the constituents' letters to the relevant department of state, with less attention to
the individual case. Only occasionally would the MP consider the more
time-consuming and arduous techniques; they are employed at a later
stage and in considerably fewer cases. An exception to this rationale is
the infrequent use of the Parliamentary Commissioner, despite the
comparative ease of invoking his assistance. The Commissioner's low
'effectiveness' would have to be the overwhelming consideration
amongst MPs. The literature on the Commissioner confirms this view
and shows evidence of diminishing use amongst MPs as they realized
the limited role that he could perform.[41]

Another major consideration by Members in their choice of
methods must be whether to make the case party political. In the great
majority of cases this is simply not possible, or at least would appear
very odd. Without doubt it is in the constituent's best interest to keep
the case out of the political debate and this would mean keeping it
away from the Parliamentary techniques, so closely tied to the party
political struggle. Thus whether the MP chooses to use the Chamber
may depend on his motives. Does he want to highlight the case to
embarrass the government or is he acting in the constituent's best
interests? Rarely will the constituent get satisfaction through resorting
immediately to a parliamentary question.

Members' comments on their constituency work confirm all these
suggestions. George Strauss MP, in an otherwise pessimistic assessment of the influence of a backbencher, observed: 'True, he has been
able, through correspondence with Ministers, to remedy a number of
grievances on behalf of his constituents.'[42] Significantly the use of
letters to ministers is the only method mentioned by Strauss. Fred
Willey MP did his own survey of his constituency work: 'In nearly
every case, I have felt that I have got a square deal in the end, although
sometimes it has been only the result of dogged persistence and
sometimes by the threat of raising the matter on the floor of the
House.'[43]

'Dogged persistence' seems to be the pestering of ministers and
officials in non-parliamentary circumstances, with the threat of
parliamentary action to follow. Bryan Gould MP also distinguished
between the letter to a minister and parliamentary techniques. He saw
the letter as the most useful and frequent course of action, especially
when the problem arises in the context of existing law and policy. The
parliamentary procedures were used later, and were most valuable as
'part of a concerted campaign on a particular issue'.[44] Paul Rose MP
also used the parliamentary procedures to conclude his campaign, not

to start it. He first sent letters to ministers, then exhausted oral and written questions. However, he had a novel use for adjournment debates, where he developed a coherent argument based on the information gained during his campaign, and sometimes published it as a pamphlet, thereby gaining a good local response and a good local press coverage.[45]

There is nothing new in the use of letters to ministers to deal with constituents' cases. Their significance today lies in their quantity in comparison with other methods of redress, and of late their greatly increased use. MPs have suggested that the major increase has been since the war,[46] with indications of significant growth in the 1960s and 1970s,[47] with the growth of community politics. The main statistical evidence of this increase is the study by Couzens of the letters handled by the Financial Secretary to the Treasury, which demonstrated a five-fold increase in correspondence with Members. In 1938 the Financial Secretary wrote 610 letters to MPs, whereas by 1954 the total had risen to 3,349. Similarly a study of Post Office parliamentary questions showed an increase from 2,000 letters in 1936 to 5,000 in 1948.[48] Many of these increases have particular and short-term explanations, but the undoubted long-term trends have important consequences for relations between administrators, representatives and the public. Closer study of the increases would also reveal the consequences of the expansion of existing services, the transfer of local services to national government, and the general growth of the welfare state.

In conclusion we can see that faced with an increasing demand for constituency services, MPs have responded by using personal correspondence with ministers. The use of parliamentary questions has increased but not in proportion to the very great increase in responsibilities and activities (and consequent mistakes) of government departments. Members do not write letters now when they previously asked questions: the great increase in the demands for constituency services has been answered by the use of correspondence with ministers. Now such correspondence is the most popular and effective means of seeking redress of grievances, the 'most important device available to Members to fulfil the function of specific representation'.[49] The increase in correspondence is a change so large as to amount to a change in kind and has become in recent years a significant new factor in government.[50]

Constituency Casework and the Functioning of Government

How does such casework contribute to the better functioning of the House of Commons? Philip Norton has noted that the liaison that results from MP-to-minister correspondence has great benefits for MPs and ministers in terms of education, as a safety valve, as a legitimizer, and as a barometer of public and parliamentary opinion.[51] The important factor in these functions is that the contact that results from constituency work is regular and convenient. The educative value for the departments is that they can discover the quality of the services they are administering and the effects of their legislation. The quality of these services are often difficult to assess from the top as only the lower levels of the services are involved with the public. Ministers can also learn a great deal about the workings of their departments through the complaints made against them. They learn not only the administrative rules that are being applied, but also how they are being applied: the quality of the services.

Norton sees the legitimizing function performed by the constituency MP as a reaction to the popular theory that MPs do not scrutinize legislation prior to legitimizing government measures, a factor which undermines the legitimacy of the House in many eyes. Here the MP is the means through which a constituent may raise grievances against legislation, and the MP thereby helps to 'shore up the electors' perceptions of its legitimacy'.[52] MPs seem to be aware of this and when faced with the possibility that the Parliamentary Commissioner would take this role away, they demanded that access should only be through MPs. As a result MPs could use the new office, not vice versa, thereby protecting 'the traditional role of Members of Parliament and their relations with the public'.[53]

The value of correspondence as a safety valve and as a barometer of public opinion are linked. It is also an excellent method of determining parliamentary opinion. Thus, once departments know what parliamentarians are concerned about, they also have an idea of the concerns of the general public. In this way constituency work can be 'one of the main motive forces for change, for revision of law, for extension of service'.[54] It also keeps the administration working on an individual basis, always mindful of the effects of an action not on social classes, or economic groups, but on individuals.

Constituency work is thus part of wider 'questions related to the linkages of Parliament to its constituencies, to its constituent, legitimising or consent mobilising functions'.[55] Doing such work the MP is responding to the demands of constituents and engaging in a mutually beneficial exchange. Belief in the MP, and the conviction that he will help if needed, has wider implications for 'diffuse support'. Almond and Verba demonstrated that an individual's access to government, here obtained through constituency work, and the belief that he can influence a government decision affect his level of activity in society and his allegiance to and the perceived legitimacy of that society. The self-confident citizen is more active, follows politics, discusses politics, and is more partisan and satisfied with his role as participant. In addition he is more favourably disposed towards the performance of his political system and generally has more positive orientations. In general satisfaction increases with participation.[56]

These factors underline the importance of the MP acting as a middle man between the citizen and central government, and the central position of constituency work in fulfilling this function. Most British citizens expect equal treatment in local and central government services, and the actions of MPs on behalf of their constituents contribute substantially to that end. The MP is the only electoral link between the periphery and centre, a strategically placed intermediary who for many constituents caters for their only demands on the system.

The role of the constituency MP is important in fact and theory. The MP acts as a safety valve for potentially escalating grievances, and as a most frequent point of entry into the state's grievance machinery. Acting thus is a traditional function of British MPs, which gives to the constituent the psychological benefits of a sense of proximity to his Member of Parliament. This was well noted by Dinnage in her study of an MP's advice bureau; she remarked on the quasi-symbolic significance of the fortnightly surgery 'where the British citizen can go to see his Parliamentary representative about his blocked drains. It symbolises the availability of "them" to "us"; it is the area where the individual, actually or in theory, has a direct line to where the action is.'[57]

The function of the constituency Member is not simply to change a few administrative decisions or to get favoured treatment for his or her constituents. The benefits come from explaining decisions, preventing disaffection, and simply being available. In doing this the constituency Member of Parliament contributes greatly to the better functioning of Parliament in particular and the British political system in general.

Notes

1 B. E. Cain, 'Partisanship and Constituency Representation' (California Institute of Technology: mimeo, n.d.) p. 12, quoting I. Crewe in *The Times Guide to the House of Commons May 1979* (London: Times Books, 1979).

2 J. Curtice and M. Steed, 'The Analysis of Voting', in D. Butler and D. Kavanagh, *The British General Election of 1979* (London: Macmillan, 1980), pp. 408–9.

3 P. Norton, *The Commons in Perspective* (Oxford: Martin Robertson, 1981), ch. 4.

4 See I. Crewe, 'Electoral Reform and the Local MP', in S. E. Finer (ed.), *Adversary Politics and Electoral Reform* (London: Wigram, 1975), p. 322, and table 2, p. 323.

5 B. E. Cain, J. A. Ferejohn, M. P. Fiorina, 'The Roots of Legislator Popularity in Great Britain and the United States', *California Institute of Technology*, *Social Science Working Paper 288* (October 1979).

6 R. Dinnage, 'Parliamentary Advice Bureau', *New Society*, 24 February 1972, p. 393.

7 See F. Morrell, *From the Electors of Bristol* (Nottingham: Spokesman Books, 1977). Morrell compares the role of 'powerful friend', where the MP is asked to help in an individual case, and the MP as an 'information exchange'. A total of 635 requests were made of the 'powerful friend', p. 29. In comparison 275 cases involved 'information exchange'. Of these, 62 involved information being sent to the MP, 94 sought information, and 119 involved the correspondent explaining political views, pp. 25–7, 28–9. The total in the area of 'information exchange' is comparatively high as it includes communications from companies etc. The important figure for comparative purposes is 119, those constituents expressing their own political opinions.
See also R. Munroe, 'The Constituency Role of Members of Parliament, With Particular Reference to the Constituency of Stoke-on-Trent (Central)' (unpublished MA thesis, University of Keele, 1975), pp. 129, 148–9. Munroe gives a very general breakdown of the postbag; the figures were: Personal 78.9 per cent; Local 13.0 per cent; National 8.1 per cent. Dinnage, 'Parliamentary Advice Bureau', does not even include expressions of opinion in her analysis of the reasons for constituents attending the surgery. See further A. Barker and M. Rush, 'Members' Postbags', in D. Leonard and V. Herman (eds), *The Backbencher and Parliament* (London: Macmillan, 1972), p. 32.

8 R. E. Dowse, 'The MP and His Surgery', *Political Studies*, 11, 1963, p. 388.

9 P. Rose, *Backbencher's Dilemma* (London: Frederick Muller, 1981), p. 77.

10 A. Beith, 'The MP as a Grievance Chaser', *Public Administration Bulletin*, 21, August 1976, p. 10. See also the review article, W. Waldegrave, *The*

Times Educational Supplement, 18 September 1981. In appealing for better research facilities for MPs in their constituency work, he notes: 'Might we not find the Executive dealing with Members not only better equipped on the policy side, but also armed with more hard examples from life?'

11 Beith, 'The MP as a Grievance Chaser', p. 10.

12 A. Barker and M. Rush, *The Member of Parliament and His Information*, (London: George Allen & Unwin, 1970), p. 194.

13 G. Strauss, 'The Influence of the Backbencher', *Political Quarterly*, 36, 1965, p. 287.

14 Barker and Rush, *The Member of Parliament and His Information*, cited by Munroe, 'The Constituency Role of Members of Parliament', pp. 122–5.

15 That correspondence is the dominant means of contact was demonstrated by Morrell, *From the Electors of Bristol*, who studied the constituency mail of Tony Benn over a calendar year, and noted that 85 per cent of the cases were handled by mail alone. Munroe, 'The Constituency Role of Members of Parliament', found that 60 per cent of cases were handled by correspondence. Dowse, 'The MP and His Surgery', found that of a choice of four means of contact, 31 out of 35 Conservative MPs cited letters, whilst 18 out of 33 Labour MPs did likewise.

16 The exception is the study by D. Samuels, 'The Member's Representation of His Constituents' Interests' (University of Hull Politics Department, third-year undergraduate dissertation, May 1981). Here the MPs under study were all of a kind most likely to attract large amounts of correspondence, i.e. well known, liberal, committed to constituency work, and representing urban seats. It is unclear whether these figures include constituency and external mail.

17 J. P. Mackintosh, 'The Changing Role of the MP: Introduction', in J. P. Mackintosh (ed.), *People and Parliament* (Farnborough: Saxon House, 1978), p. 77. Again Dowse, 'The MP and His Surgery', found no indication that marginality affected the tendency to hold surgeries. However, B. Cain, J. Ferejohn and M. Fiorina, 'The House is Not a Home', *Legislative Studies Quarterly*, 4(4), Nov. 1979, p. 33, concludes from their limited sample: 'Not surprisingly those who believe that constituency service will have a large effect on their electoral future allocate more effort to it.'

18 B. E. Cain, J. A. Ferejohn, and M. P. Fiorina, 'Popular Evaluations of Representatives in Great Britain and the United States' (California Institute of Technology: mimeo, n.d.), table 3, p. 16.

19 Ibid., p. 18.

20 J. Jeger, 'The Image of the MP', in Mackintosh, *People and Parliament*, pp. 12–15.

21 Crewe, 'Electoral Reform', p. 322.

22 See Morrell, *From the Electors of Bristol*, and Munroe, 'The Constituency Role of Members of Parliament'.

23 Beith, The MP as a Grievance Chaser', p. 8.

24 Cain, 'Partisanship and Constituency Representation', p. 7.

25 Ibid.

26 P. M. Williams, 'The MP's Personal Vote', *Parliamentary Affairs*, 1966–67, p. 26.

27 A. M. Rees and T. A. Smith, *Town Councillors* (London: Acton Trust Society, 1964), pp. 46–7.

28 Ibid, p. 113.

29 Maud Committee on the Management of Local Government, vol. 2, *The Local Government Councillor* (London: HMSO, 1967).

30 H. Heclo, 'The Councillor's Job', *Public Administration*, 47(2), Summer, 1969.

31 Ibid, p. 190.

32 Graham Page, Minister for Local Government and Development, *HC Deb.* 826, col. 348.

33 Samuels, 'The Member' Representation of His Constituents' Interests'

34 W. Hampton, *Democracy and Community* (London: Oxford University Press, 1970), p. 77; Munroe, 'The Constituency Role of Members of Parliament', p. 89. The Stoke-on-Trent survey revealed that 50.4 per cent of cases handled by the MP were concerned with local government matters.

35 R. Munroe, 'The Member of Parliament as Representative: The View from the Constituency', *Political Studies*, 25(4), p. 34.

36 Hampton, *Democracy and Community*, p. 87; B. E. Cain, J. A. Ferejohn and M. P. Fiorina, 'Assessing Constituency Involvement: The Hemel Hempstead Experience' (California Institute of Technology: mimeo, n.d.), p. 15.

37 Munroe, 'The Constituency Role of Members of Parliament', p. 105.

38 J. Bonner, 'Public Interest in Local Government', *Public Administration*, 32, 1952. For confirmation of this view see Rees and Smith, *Town Councillors* p. 47. For an alternative view see A. H. Birch, *Small Town Politics* (London: Oxford University Press, 1959), where greater numbers were aware of their councillors. Rees and Smith felt that Birch's findings differed regarding knowledge of and contact with their councillors, as Glossop was so much smaller than Barking, the town which they studied.

39 Except with the Parliamentary Commissioner for Administration, who can only be contacted through the MP.

40 R. Gregory and A. Alexander, 'Our Parliamentary Ombudsman. Pt 2: Development and the Problem of Identity', *Public Administration*, 51(1), 1973, p. 48.

41 L. H. Cohen, 'The Parliamentary Commissioner and the MP Filter', *Public Law*, 1972, using information from a questionnaire to 620 MPs, and 152 ex-MPs, sitting after 1967. Only 7 out of 194 referred cases to the PCA immediately: p. 210.

42 Strauss, 'The Influence of the Backbencher', p. 287.

43 F. Willey, *The Honourable Member* (London: Sheldon Press, 1974), p. 155.

44 B. Gould, 'The MP and Constituency Cases', in Mackintosh, *People and Parliament*, p. 87.

45 Rose, *Backbencher's Dilemma*, p. 96.
46 Barker and Rush, *The Member of Parliament and His Information*, p. 25.
47 Rose, *Backbencher's Dilemma*, p. 25.
48 K. Couzens, 'A Minister's Correspondence', *Public Administration*, 34(3), 1956, pp. 237–44. A. Phillips, 'Post Office Parliamentary Questions', *Public Administration*, 27(2), Summer 1949, pp. 91–9.
49 P. Norton, 'Dear Minister . . . An Analysis of MP to Minister Correspondence', paper delivered to the Political Studies Association Conference, April 1981, p. 25.
50 Couzens, 'A Minister's Correspondence', p. 242.
51 Norton, 'Dear Minister', p. 13.
52 Ibid., p. 23.
53 R. Gregory and A. Alexander, 'Our Parliamentary Ombudsman: Pt 1: Integration and Metamorphosis', *Public Administration*, 50(3), 1972, p. 326.
54 Beith, 'The MP as a Grievance Chaser', p. 10.
55 S. Patterson, 'The British House of Commons as a Focus for Political Research', *British Journal of Political Science*, 3, July 1973, p. 380.
56 G. Almond and S. Verba, *The Civic Culture* (Boston, Mass.: Little, Brown, 1965), p. 206; also table VIII, p. 199.
57 Dinnage, 'Parliamentary Advice Bureau', p. 393.

Part II

The House of Lords

5

Behavioural Changes

A New Professionalism and a More Independent House

Nicholas D. J. Baldwin

Many tenets of conventional wisdom exist about the House of Lords. We are told, for example, that there is a large, permanent, inbuilt majority for one political party – the Conservative Party – among the membership; that the overwhelming majority of members, whether in receipt of the Conservative Party whip or not, are certainly conservative and more likely reactionary in their outlook; that there exists a body of these reactionary peers, known as backwoodsmen, who have either never attended sittings of the House or have seldom done so, but who nonetheless could do so at the drop of a hat – or at least at the crack of a whip – and have a decisive influence on the outcome of divisions; that, in short, the Conservative Party, be it in government or opposition, has complete control over, and can impose its will upon, the House.

Conservative dominance within the Lords was a product of history. At the beginning of the eighteenth century there had been a very small majority in the House for the Whigs. This had then been turned into an even smaller Tory majority by the creation of 12 peers for the specific purpose of securing a majority for the ratification of the Treaty of Utrecht in 1712. After a few years the Whigs were once again in a majority, a position they were able to maintain until Pitt the Younger became Prime Minister (1783), when creations took place on an unprecedented scale – during the 17 years of his premiership 140 peerages were created, providing the Tories not merely with a majority, but placing them in a position of ascendancy in the House of Lords. This ascendancy was underlined by the natural conservative tendencies of an hereditary House and was increased by defections from amongst Liberal peers as a result of the infusion of radically minded individuals into the Liberal Party as a whole. In 1868 the

House contained a majority opposed to the Liberal government of between 60 and 70, and although a number of Liberal creations took place, they in fact did little more than compensate for defections which occurred. The events of 1886 and the issue of Irish Home Rule drove the great majority of Liberal peers to join the Conservatives, and the strength of the Liberal government in the Lords was believed to be as little as 30. The actual strength was put to the test in 1893 with the vote on Gladstone's second Home Bill. It showed a majority of nearly 400 – 419 to 41 – against the government. By 1906 the membership of the House entitled to participate in proceedings stood at 602. Of these only 88 described themselves as Liberals, and in reality a number of these were extremely dubious supporters of the newly elected Liberal government. There were 355 Conservatives and 124 Liberal Unionists, which left only 35, including 14 bishops and a number of Princes of the Blood Royal, who had no political label. Hence there was at that time in the House of Lords a nominal Unionist majority of 391; Conservative dominance was a fact. Conservative dominance was complete following the Labour election victory in 1945, for the government party was supported by as few as 18 members within the House of Lords.

It is apparent, therefore, that the traditional concepts outlined have their origins in fact. Their preponderance became not merely the accepted, but the unchallenged norm. Their continued exposition, however, ignores an important – possibly the most important – aspect of the British constitution, namely its capacity for gradually adapting itself to meet changing conditions. Throughout history the British constitution has been adapting itself to its environment. Transitions have as a rule been gradual, deference to tradition habitual, and there has been a tendency to maintain throughout accustomed names and forms, to the extent that the constitutional history of Britain displays an unparalleled continuity.

In this respect the House of Lords is but a microcosm of the British constitution, for throughout it is apparent that it has been able to adapt to meet the changing conditions within which it has found itself functioning. This is so because, in contrast to other present-day second chambers which have been specially created institutions, with their powers and compositions clearly defined in constitutional documents and whose origins can be traced to some theoretical and practical purpose in the minds of those responsible for drawing up the constitution, the House of Lords was not established to meet the requirement of any particular theory of politics; it was not created by any national convention; it does not owe its existence to some paper scheme drawn up by politicians, academics or constitutional lawyers. Rather it is a product of history. It has not been made; it has grown. Herein lies the key to why the House of Lords, this curious institution which has been the subject of a protracted, often ritual, campaign of abuse, is still in existence; the key to why it has not only remained, in essence, untouched by the hand of whole-scale reform, but also to why it has not fallen victim to inward decay; the key to why the House of Lords can correctly be depicted as the perennial survivor. It is because it has an inherent evolutionary adaptability. This is not to say that this evolution has been a neat continuous one; on the contrary, its development has been haphazard, spasmodic, irregular and uncertain. Nonetheless, from the beginning it has developed organically, gradually modifying, often indiscernibly, both the attitudes and behaviour of its participatory membership and its own procedures in response to the prevailing circumstances.

In recent years this evolutionary adaptability has resulted in significant changes in both composition and behaviour. Today, although the House of Lords appears essentially unchanged from that which existed 10, 20, 30, even 40 years ago, in practice fundamental changes of both form and character have taken place, to the extent that many of the commonly held beliefs that have been applied to the House of Lords have in effect been rendered incorrect. The fact is, however, that because the House of Lords has throughout been able to retain its identity, the changes that have taken place have gone largely unrecognized, so that perceptions of what the position is thought to be have not kept pace with what the position is in practice. The result of this is that contemporary arguments and observations on the subject of the House of Lords portray a tendency to ignore changes in both composition and behaviour that have taken place in recent years, and instead reiterate and re-emphasize the traditional received ideas. These changes, as highlighted by events since 1979, provide clear evidence not only of the development of what is a new professionalism and a new independence amongst the membership, but also, and as a result, of the fallaciousness of much of the conventional wisdom associated with the subject.

The House since 1979

With the return of a Conservative government in 1979, backed by a solid Commons majority, it was assumed by many that the House of Lords would be little noticed. In fact, however, the reverse has been the case, it having been made abundantly clear since 1979 that the days when a Conservative government need have no fear of being defeated in the Lords have disappeared. Indeed, by the middle of 1984, the talk had become that of the House of Lords providing the most effective opposition to the government, the Lords being the focus of much of the opposition to the government's rate-capping scheme and its plans to abolish the Greater London Council and the six metropolitan county councils.

During the first parliamentary session under the Conservative administration elected in 1979, the government was able to avoid being defeated on any significant legislative matter on the floor of the House of Commons. It was not able, however, to avoid such defeats in the House of Lords. The most notable of these occurred when the Lords objected to a clause in the Education (No. 2) Bill which would have enabled local authorities to impose charges for school transport, and voted by 216 votes to 112 to delete it. The division not merely saw two former Conservative Ministers of Education, Lords Butler and Boyle, vote against the government, but saw a total of 38 Conservative peers walk into the lobby in opposition to the government, a total of 28.7 per cent of all Conservatives voting. This division went a long way to emphasize the change in the political balance that has gradually evolved in the House in recent years. In a division which saw a high degree of activity by the government whips and which saw a high turnout of members voting (itself a factor which conventional wisdom has as favouring the Conservatives), it is interesting to point out that even if all those Conservatives voting against the government had instead followed the party whip, the government would still have been defeated by 22 votes. In addition, even if all the Conservative peers, supported by all those peers with no declared party allegiance who voted in this division, had gone through the same division lobby, the government would still have been defeated by 13 votes. The sheer scale of this defeat, with the prospect of having to face backbench dissent in the Commons and a second defeat if put before the Lords again, encouraged the government to climb down.

A further indication of the evolutionary changes in the political environment found in the House of Lords was provided by its dealings with regard to the Employment Bill during the 1979–80 session. The Bill embodied the step-by-step approach to trade-union immunities against legal action favoured by the then Employment Secretary, James Prior. The Bill was the subject of a campaign by the right wing of the Conservative Party whose intent was to toughen the Bill by outlawing all secondary industrial action. The House of Lords was viewed by the campaigners as the place in which amendments to this effect would be passed, given the traditional view that the House of Lords is dominated not merely by conservative but by reactionary peers. The attempt came with an amendment to clause 17 (the clause which gave continued immunity to some classes of secondary action) which sought to outlaw all secondary action. This attempt, however, was overwhelmingly defeated by 249 votes to 41.

Additional evidence of the changing nature of the political balance that existed in the House of Lords was provided during proceedings on the Housing Bill, again during the 1979–80 session, when the government suffered a series of defeats. The most significant of these occurred when the Lords voted by 109 to 74 to exclude council homes built for old people from the Bill's right to-buy provisions. Although the government indicated that it had no intention of accepting this amendment, following considerable public and private protest by the peers this was precisely what it did. The important factor which brought about such a change in the government's position was the awareness, brought home by the peers' protests, that were the matter returned to the Lords, they would have insisted on their original amendment being reinstated. Facing this situation and the resulting possibility that the entire Bill could be lost due to the lack of time as the end of the session approached, the government accepted the amendment, thereby enabling the Bill to reach the statute book before the session ended.

The following session provided further evidence of the changing nature of the House as the government was once again defeated on a number of occasions, including over an important amendment to the British Nationality Bill – an amendment according a special right to citizens of Gibraltar to register as British citizens being carried by 150 votes to 112. This defeat led, for the first time under a Conservative government, to veiled hints of a possible constitutional crisis, Lord Aylestone (Social Democrat) warning that, were the government to overturn the Gibraltar amendment, 'maybe we shall have a constitutional problem here the like of which we have not seen for a very long time,'[1] while Lord Boyd-Carpenter (Conservative) remarked:

I do not know what the Government's intentions in [the House of Commons] may be in respect of the Gibraltar amendment. . . . This is a matter on which some of us . . . feel very strongly. . . . [It has been] suggested that if the Government acted foolishly in this matter there might be a constitutional crisis. There will be nothing of the sort. If the Government like to wait a year and use the machinery of the Parliament Act they can get their way, but, of course, this particular Bill would be lost.[2]

Hence, the government had been warned that any successful attempt to reverse the Gibraltar amendment in the House of Commons would only then be met by a hostile reception in the Lords; a warning supported by the government's own soundings of the situation. In order to secure the passage of the legislation that session, the government chose to accept the amendment.

A string of other defeats has followed, including, for example, a defeat on the Telecommunication Bill, which forced the government to pledge to introduce legislation to regulate 'phone tapping; on an amendment to the Police and Criminal Evidence Bill to the effect that only police officers in uniform be allowed to stop and search suspects; on an amendment to the Trades Union Bill requiring union executives to be elected by postal ballot; three defeats on the Housing and Building Control Bill excluding houses owned by charities and those specially adapted for the elderly and the disabled from the right-to-buy provisions; and, most recently, defeats on the Ordnance Factories and Military Services Bill.[3] The most far-reaching defeat, however, was inflicted upon the government's plan to cancel the May 1985 elections to the Greater London Council and the six metropolitan county councils, replacing them with nominated interim councils in preparation for their abolition in 1986, which came before the House as the Local Government (Interim Provisions) Bill in June 1984. An all-party amendment whose effect was to allow the elections to go ahead, thus ripping the heart out of the Bill, was carried against the government by 191 votes to 143, an anti-Government majority of 48;[4] a defeat made all the more striking by the fact that it occurred in the face of concerted government whipping. Indeed, as was observed at the time, 'One of the principal consequences of [this] remarkable vote ... has been to shatter the conventional wisdom on the House of Lords.'[5]

Hence, since the return of the Conservatives to government in 1979, the House of Lords has by no means been subservient to Conservative wishes. There is clear evidence that Conservative government concern over not being able to secure the passage of particular items of legislation in a particular session has been at least a factor in persuading ministers to accept unpalatable amendments and to reach compromises on a number of occasions during the post-1979 period. Indeed, one of the salient features of the work of the Lords with regard to legislation during this period has been the new phenomenon of their growing assertiveness, not merely to amend legislation emanating from a Conservative government, but to change it considerably. In short, and as highlighted by the fact that since 1979 the Conservative government has been defeated on more than 60 occasions (45 defeats

in the 1979–83 Parliament and 19 in the present Parliament up to July
1984), the modern House of Lords increasingly is prepared to create
difficulties for Conservative governments – a fact in clear contraven-
tion of the tenets of conventional wisdom. Why is this so? What has
brought such a change about?

Analysis

During the years immediately after the passage of the Reform Act of
1832 the House of Lords acted in a way which gave rise to little
conflict between the two Houses. However, towards the latter half of
the nineteenth century, until 1914, it is difficult to describe its activities
other than in terms of conflict between the Unionist opinions and
landed interests which were prevalent among peers at the time and the
Liberal majorities in the House of Commons. Indeed, as the policies
advocated by the Liberal government became increasingly objection-
able to the established interests represented by Conservatives in the
Lords the conflict became sharper, precipitating the constitutional
crisis of 1909–11. The settlement of that crisis came with the passage
of the Parliament Act of 1911. The significance of this Act was
two-fold. Firstly, it created procedures whereby obstruction by the
Lords could be overcome, and secondly, and more importantly, it
served to act as a deterrent to obstruction by the Lords. It is upon these
twin pillars that the activities of the Lords have evolved and developed
since 1911, to the extent that today the reform, challenged at its
inception as undermining the entire constitutional edifice of the
nation, can be regarded as one of the very cornerstones of that
constitutional edifice. It can be seen as such because, more through
gradual evolution than by design, it led to the development of a
chamber which is neither too dependent nor too independent, which
has influence but not authority. This was not, however, self-evident at
the time.

Although assertive during the period of 1911 to 1914, the onset of
the war followed by a long period in which the Conservative Party, save
for two brief intervals, was the dominant element in government
precipitated a state of quiescence on the part of the Lords. The
election of a Labour government in 1945 did not shake the peers from
this state, a state which owed much to the fact that the peers were
waiting for their House to be reformed – the preamble to the
Parliament Act of 1911 having stated that it was intended only as a
temporary measure, a stop-gap, before a thoroughgoing reform to

substitute for the House of Lords a second chamber constituted on a popular instead of a hereditary basis could be carried out. Although a number expected the 1945 Labour government to initiate such a scheme, it was not until after the return of a Labour government following the general election of 1966 that a serious attempt at reform was instigated, firm proposals based upon inter-party talks being brought forward as the Parliament (No. 2) Bill during the 1968–9 session. The proposals involved, however, received a critical and, in some respects, hostile reception in the House of Commons, in large part because they were perceived as a means of making the Lords more effective (and thereby likely to have more authority and ability to use their powers), and the legislation was ultimately dropped. Because of the circumstances surrounding the collapse of this attempt at whole-scale reform – the perception being that the government had had its fingers burned – the subject of reform came to be regarded as an issue governments would be hesitant to get involved with again, and as such was seen as having been placed on the 'back-burner'.

The episode had a profound effect on many of the peers. The position, as they saw it, was that they remained unreformed through no fault of their own (to a very great extent they had favoured the reforms proposed), while the circumstances of the collapse made it apparent that they were likely to remain unreformed at least for the foreseeable future. As one member explained: 'The failure of the [reform] proposals had the effect of freeing us from the lethargy that had encumbered and inhibited us for so long. From this point we were determined not to pussy-foot about any longer but instead to get on with the job in hand'.[6]

This attitude was not simply a reaction to events; rather, it was the result of a number of changes that had taken place during the intervening years. The most important of these was the addition of life peers to the membership following the passage of the Life Peerages Act in 1958. The effect upon the composition of the House was marked, as table 5.1 demonstrates. Lloyd George had described hereditary peers as 'Dug out of the cellars of the House of Lords . . . stuff bottled in the Dark Ages . . . not fit to drink . . . cobwebby, dusty, muddy, sour'.[7] The innovation of peerages for life proved to be an ingenious method whereby, continuing the analogy, old bottles were filled with new wine, and as such had a significant effect on the House. As one hereditary peer explained, 'there was a tremendous revival. . . . Looking back [it can be said that] the Life Peerages Act really saved [the] House as an entity, and for its future. . . . [because] it injected considerable new life into the work of the House.'[38]

Table 5.1   Composition of the House of Lords, 1950–1984

Type of peerage	1950 N	1950 %	1960 N	1960 %	1970 N	1970 %	June 1984 N	June 1984 %
Created hereditary peer	810	95.6	843	92.8	97	9.0	30	2.5
Hereditary by succession (male)					741	68.7	745	62.6
Hereditary by succession (female)	–	–	–	–	19	1.8	18	1.5
Life peer (male)	–	–	31	3.4	155	14.4	305	25.6
Life peeresses	–	–			23	2.1	46	3.9
Law lord	11	1.3	8	0.9	17	1.6	20	1.7
Lords spiritual	26	3.1	26	2.9	26	2.4	26	2.2
Total	847	100.0	908	100.0	1,078	100.0	1,190	100.0

Although today the 'popular' view of the House of Lords is of a place full of landed aristocrats up from their country estates, mainstream politicians of a bygone age, wealthy patrons of party funds, friends of former Prime Ministers and titled fugitives from the pages of P. G. Wodehouse, to portray the membership in such terms would be inaccurate. The addition of a large number of life peers, although not fundamentally altering the nature of the composition of the House (as, for example, direct elections would have done), has enriched it by bringing in members of more varied backgrounds and experiences (see table 5.2). Since the passage of the Life Peerages Act the House of Lords has acquired newly ennobled bankers, engineers, diplomats, lawyers, businessmen, economists, trade unionists, military commanders, politicians, academics, educationalists, scientists, administrators and senior civil servants, on a scale unprecedented before the passage of the Act. As a result of this blend of hereditary and life peers, the House has members with very considerable knowledge of almost every aspect of life. There are peers with personal knowledge of all parts of the world, from Grenada and the Falklands to the Soviet Union and China; there are peers who have climbed mountains and others who

Table 5.2   House of Lords: occupational experience 1981

| | | Percentage of peerage category | |
| | | | Created/ |
Occupation	N	Hereditary	appointed
Full-time trade union official	20	–	4.9
Civil/diplomatic service	114	6.2	16.1
Legal (judge/barrister/solicitor)	120	5.9	18.3
Banking/insurance	121	11.6	7.8
Engineer	25	1.6	3.2
Accountant/economist	25	1.9	2.4
Scientist	9	0.4	1.5
Medical (surgeon/doctor/ dentist)	19	0.6	3.4
Teaching (school/university)	103	3.4	18.8
Industry	208	15.6	21.5
Politics	166	3.0	34.9
Total	1,178		

have worked down mines; there are peers who are shopkeepers and there are peers who are chairmen of the largest chain stores; there are policemen, ex-prisoners and former Home Secretaries; there are bankers and there are those who have been bankrupt; there are civil service clerks and there are civil service mandarins; there are peers from palaces and there are peers from council houses. Indeed, there are peers from almost all walks of life:

The wide composition of the House is in itself a source of strength. . . . if any odd and bizarre subject comes up – let us say, potato-growing in Peru . . . – you will find arriving in the House some noble lord . . . who in the early part of his life engaged in potato-growing in Peru. . . . The fact that such people . . . come and give us first-hand information of their experience is . . . of great value to us.[9]

Because this is the case, it has become the custom for only experts or at least people with considerable knowledge to speak on specialized subjects. This leads to a very high level of debate. Certainly it is difficult – though admittedly not impossible – to find a topic for debate on which there is not at least one peer (and, more often than not, several peers) who is either a recognized authority or at least has considerable practical knowledge, and today any major debate in the

House is *likely* to include speeches from experts. An analysis of participants in debates on subjects ranging from Afghanistan to zoology underlines this. Take but one example: education. A considerable number of peers have experience in the education sector. The then Minister of State, Baroness Young, called attention to this fact when moving the Second Reading of the Education Bill in 1980, noting 'there are no fewer than eighteen former Ministers in this House, and of these eight occupied a position equivalent to that of the Secretary of State today.'[10] The extent of this knowledge and expertise can be seen when the participants in one debate are examined, in this instance the debate on expenditure cuts in education, held on 18 March 1981. The debate brought contributions from 25 speakers in all. Table 5.3 reveals the extent of their grounding in the subject.

Table 5.3   Participants in Lords' education debate, 18 March 1981

Peer	Experience in education sector
Lord Swann (life peer 1981)	Chancellor of York University
Lord Oram (life peer 1976)	Former teacher
Baroness Derrington (life peeress 1978)	Former teacher
Lord Vaizey (life peer 1976)	Professor of economics, Brunel University; member of the Public Schools Commission 1966–8
Lord James of Rusholme (life peer 1959)	High Master, Manchester Grammar School 1945–61; Vice-Chancellor, University of York, 1962–73
Lord Donaldson of Kingsbridge (life peer 1967)	Minister of State, Education, 1976–9
Lord Kaldor (life peer 1974)	Former Professor of economics, Cambridge University; special adviser to Chancellors of Exchequer during Labour governments (1964–8, 1974–6)
Lord Alexander of Potterhill (life peer 1974)	General Secretary of the Association of Educational Committees 1945–77
Earl of Longford (created peer 1945)	Former school teacher and lecturer at the London School of Economics
Lord Davies of Leek (life peer 1970)	Former schoolmaster and tutor in adult education

Table 5.3   continued

Peer	Experience in education sector
Lord Harris of High Cross (life peer 1979)	Formerly lecturer in political economy, St Andrew's University, and Director General of the Institute of Economic Affairs
Lord Segal (life peer 1964)	Former chairman of the National Society for Mentally Handicapped Children
Lord Annan (life peer 1965)	Vice-Chancellor, University of London
Baroness Seear (life peeress 1971)	Reader and teacher at the London School of Economics
Lord Stewart of Fulham (life peer 1979)	Former teacher and lecturer for Workers Education Association; former Secretary of State for Education
Lord Flowers (life peer 1979)	Rector of the Imperial College of Science and Technology
Lord Ritchie-Calder (life peer 1966)	Professor of international relations, Edinburgh University, 1961–7
Lord Perry of Walton (life peer 1979)	Professor of pharmacology, University of Edinburgh, 1958–68, and Vice-Chancellor, Open University, 1969–80

The introduction of life peers has also gradually caused the style of the House to alter, particularly because a number – a growing number – of the new creations have been 'working peers', individuals created peers with the specific task of being working legislators, distinguishing them from those names which appear in the Honours Lists at the New Year and on the Queen's Birthday. Many of the life peers have been MPs or have been active in local government or party politics, and as such have tended to approach their role as members of the Lords with a degree of professionalism previously unfamiliar to the House, and this in turn has had something of a knock-on effect among the hereditary element. This 'new professionalism' remained largely unrecognized, however, until the beginning of the 1970s, firstly because it could not materialize with any effect until a significant number of life peers had been created and secondly because the threat/promise of reform had until then been present. Since 1970 the members have approached their work in a manner and with a determination previously unknown (table 5.4).

Table 5.4   House of Lords: sessional statistics 1950–1984

Statistical item	1950/1	1960/1	1970/1	1980/1	1983/4[a]
Average daily attendance	86	142	265	296	322
Number of sitting days	100	125	153	143	164
Number of sitting hours	294.45	599	966.02	919.53	1,194.56
Average length of sitting	2.57	4.47	6.18	6.25	7.17
Sittings after 10.00 p.m.	1	5	38	53	88

[a]Up to 20 July 1984.

From table 5.4, it can be seen that the number of peers attending sittings has greatly increased; indeed, between 1950/1 and 1983/4 there has been an increase of some 370 per cent in average daily attendance, itself both a sign and a cause of the new professionalism. In addition, members are spending more and more time at the Lords and are involved in an increasing amount of business when there. Whereas peers could at one time count on a working week of Tuesday through to Thursday and a working day often not beginning until 4.00 p.m. and possibly ending before 7.00 p.m., now the House sits more often, the working week has expanded, the sittings begin earlier and go on much longer in order to accommodate the new professionalism of the membership.

In addition, the business arrangements of the House have, little by little, been adapted to meet these changes, the membership being anxious not only to improve their own procedures but to evolve existing functions and to develop new ones. The fact that the House is a self-regulating body with few standing orders (for example, it has no 'Speaker', no guillotine, no closure) has enabled the membership to do just this.

As pointed out above, changes have also taken place with regard to the political balance found amongst the membership: these are shown in table 5.5.

Table 5.5   Political affiliation of peers, 1970–1984

Party/group	1970		June 1984	
	N	%	N	%
Conservative	468	43.4	460	38.6
Labour	120	11.1	133	11.2
Liberal	38	3.5	39	3.3
Social Democrat	–	–	38	3.2
Communist	2	0.2	2	0.2
Independents – crossbench[a]	110	10.2	209	17.6
– non-party[b]	51	4.8	50	4.2
No declared political affiliation[c]	289	26.8	259	21.7
Total	1,078	100.0	1,190	100.0

[a]Those in receipt of the independent crossbench 'notification of business'.
[b]Law lords, archbishops, bishops and (some) royal dukes.
[c]Those peers about whose party allegiance no information is available.

By far the strongest political grouping in terms of numbers is the Conservative Party, though it should be noted that, in absolute and proportional terms, there has been a decline in recent years in the number of peers who are in receipt of the Conservative whip. The largest growth has been in the number of peers sitting on the crossbenches – an increase by the middle of 1984 of 90.0 per cent over the 1970 level. Also important to note is the decline in the number of peers who have no declared political or group affiliations. Similarly worthy of note has been the rise of the Social Democratic Party in the Lords. By June 1984 38 members were in receipt of that party's whip, a figure made up of 19 former Labour peers, 13 peers from the crossbenches, two former Conservatives and four who had not previously declared any political affiliation.

However, because there is a marked difference between the total possible membership and the actual achieved day-to-day membership, and because a significant number of members are not affiliated to any political party, considerable confusion exists over what the political complexion of the House of Lords is.

The outcome of any division depends upon two basic factors, namely the numbers of members voting and the way in which they cast their votes. These basic factors in turn depend upon a number of variables, such as the subject under discussion, the advocacy of certain individuals, the day of the week and the hour of the day. Any exposition of the political complexion of the House of Lords is invalidated unless it takes into account these factors. When they are taken into account, it becomes apparent that the complete Conservative control evident in 1945, indeed evident into the 1960s, has disappeared; gone are the days when a Conservative government need have no fear of defeat in the Lords. Indeed, as we have seen, the Lords have in the years since 1979 been an increasing embarrassment, irritant and obstruction to the Conservative government. As a former Conservative Leader of the House has observed, 'although in the past there was a built-in Conservative majority, at present, and at best, taking account of the factors highlighted, there is only ever a potential Conservative majority.'[11] The position now is that 'The House of Lords has a mind of its own and no single party can rely unreservedly on its support.'[12]

Alongside the shift in the political balance, there has been a change in the collective attitude of the House. It has become no longer synonymous with reaction, the peers having obtained instead a reputation for moderation, reason and tolerance; a reputation which is directly derived from their deliberations on such controversial issues as reform of the laws concerning homosexuality, divorce, abortion, the provision of free contraception and so on. Indeed, pertinent to this, it is interesting to note the extent of the change that has occurred, for although the Lords voted heavily against the abolition of the death penalty in 1956, by 1983 it was widely expected that, had the House of Commons supported the reintroduction of capital punishment, the House of Lords would have voted heavily against it.

The new professionalism, linked with the altered political balance, has meant that peers have not only recognized but have responded to political developments. In short, the House of Lords has adapted its behaviour, chameleon-like, to its changing political environment, taking into account not only the political complexion of the government with which it is faced, but also such factors as whether or not the government at a particular time or on a particular issue has a secure majority in the House of Commons, and the way in which the government of the day organizes the business timetable in both the Lords and and Commons. The House of Lords – the peers – weigh up such factors, judging how best to act and react to them. A change in one of the factors leads to corresponding changes, though often imperceptible, in their own mode of procedure.

During the 1970s, for example, the Lords were faced with three specific, though interrelated, developments in the Commons, namely minority government, a significant increase in the levels of intraparty dissent in the division lobbies, and the fact that, as a result of these two factors, government defeats were no longer infrequent occurrences. The Lords responded accordingly, using these factors to their advantage, amending legislation against the government's wishes in the hope that the amendments would receive support in the House of Commons; support which was, on a number of significant occasions, forthcoming. Because this was the case, the Lords were also able to secure compromises from the government merely by threatening to return items to the Commons, thereby placing the government in danger of being defeated – the perception being that the government would be more open to making concessions in order to avoid the risk of returning legislation to the Commons, particularly on matters where it had had considerable difficulty securing a Commons majority a first time.

During the 1980s circumstances within the House of Commons have altered in that there have been large majorities for the government. The peers have responded to this change, adapting their behaviour accordingly. The root cause of the most recent change was the result of the general election of 1983, which secured, on a minority vote, a 144-seat Commons majority for the Conservative government. This led some peers, from all sides of the House, to the conclusion that the composition of the Commons represented a distortion of public opinion and that because of the political balance in the Lords it, rather than the Commons, was, in this respect at least, more representative of public opinion. As one peer concluded: 'We have entered a very special period. The House of Commons is now so totally unrepresentative that I feel the Lords are entitled to be much less co-operative in putting Commons legislation onto the statute book'.[13] Or, as one observer noted: 'The heart of democracy [the House of Commons], pumping the blood stream round the system, has [because of the high government majority] ceased to function properly. . . . the Lords see themselves as the bypass valve, restoring health to the organism'.[14] This is indeed the way many of the peers currently view their role, and is the reason for the coming together of four groups of peers, Labour, Alliance, crossbench and dissident Conservatives, with a view to providing effective opposition – certainly effective scrutiny. Hence the series of recent defeats inflicted upon the present government by the House of Lords.

Through these changes, through its evolutionary adaptability, the House of Lords has developed a new strength and vigour, and an inner confidence in itself as an institution and in what it is doing. The constitutional confrontation between the two Houses of Parliament in the late nineteenth and early twentieth centuries was not, in essence, the result of differences between two partisan political philosophies, but was rather the result of a failure on the part of the Lords to recognize and accept the implications of the political trends of the time, namely the inevitability of the transference of political power to the elected House of Commons. It is during the past 25 years, and more especially in the years since 1970, as a direct result of the external reforms that have taken place and of the internal changes brought about by them, that the peers have fully accepted and adapted to the limitations inherent in their position; indeed 'the House of Lords is able to function today largely because its members recognise and accept the constraints within which it works.'[15]

In the process of adaptation the House of Lords has itself changed, evolving into what legislative 'revolution' has always failed to bring about, namely a more balanced second chamber. As the professionalism and independence of its members grew, so the House of Lords developed an effective capacity for influencing – though not determining – the course of events.

Conclusion

In 1867 Walter Bagehot wrote that:

the danger of the House of Lords is that ... it is not safe against inward decay. ... If most of its members neglect their duties, if all of its members continue to be of one class ... if its doors are shut against genius that cannot found a family, and ability which has not £5000 a year. ... Its danger is not in assassination, but atrophy; not abolition, but decline.[16]

A study of the House of Lords in recent years provides clear evidence that it is in danger of neither atrophy nor decline; indeed, quite the reverse becomes apparent. The House of Lords has portrayed throughout a remarkable ability to evolve and adapt to changing circumstances. What also becomes evident is its quite extraordinary character, a character derived from the fact that it is not the brainchild of any constitutional draftsman but is instead a strange amalgam of the provisions of a small number of *ad hoc* statutes, together with precedents, habits, conventions, customs, traditions, usages, understandings and beliefs. Although the House of Lords has been altered by what can be termed external measures – such as the Reform Act of 1832, the Parliament Acts of 1911 and 1949, and the Life Peerages

Act of 1958 – it has been the internal reactions to them, the capacity to adapt to the changes they heralded, that have formed and continue to shape the character of the House. The House of Lords as it exists today is the result of this evolutionary process. Certainly it is an illogical institution, to the extent that no one would set out to devise a second chamber like it, but it is its very irrationality that in a strange, even perverse, way is its strength. It encompasses a delicately balanced combination of limited effectiveness with ultimate impotence through which it is, in a rather haphazard and improbable fashion, able to make a significant contribution to the process of government.

Notes

1 Lord Aylestone, *HL Deb*. 424, col. 722 (20 October 1981).
2 Lord Boyd-Carpenter, *HL Deb*. 424, col. 731 (20 October 1981).
3 Not all these amendments have been accepted outright or accepted in modified form by the government.
4 The government offered a compromise in the face of the defeat to the effect that, although the elections of May 1985 would be cancelled, instead of replacing them by nominated interim councils the Greater London Council and the six metropolitan county councils would remain in office throughout the period prior to the passage by Parliament of an abolition Bill.
5 G. Smith, in *The Times*, 2 July 1984.
6 Labour life peer to author.
7 Lloyd George, quoted in I. Gilmour, *The Body Politic* (London: Hutchinson, 1969), p. 297.
8 Lord De Clifford, *HL Deb*. 352, col. 1104 (20 June 1974).
9 Earl Jowitt, *HL Deb*. 179, cols 527–8 (25 November 1952).
10 *HL Deb*. 405, col 1010 (25 February 1980).
11 Former Conservative Leader of the House to author.
12 Bishop to author.
13 Lord Mayhew, *Liberal News*, 2 August 1983.
14 H. Young, 'Praise the Rebel Lords But Pass the Electoral Ammunition', *The Guardian*, 9 July 1984.
15 Crossbench life peer to author.
16 W. Bagehot, *The English Constitution*, first published 1867 (London: Fontana/Collins, 1975), p. 149.

6

Structural Changes
The Use of Committees

Cliff Grantham and Caroline Moore Hodgson

In the 1950s and early 1960s, the House of Lords was essentially an amateur, poorly attended and chamber-orientated institution. The House met in a rather leisurely fashion. All scrutiny of government – and legislation – was taken on the floor of the House. There was the time so to take it; there was a lack of resources to do anything else. In the 1970s, the picture was to change significantly. There was, as was shown in the preceding chapter, a marked change in behaviour. Peers sat for longer hours; they displayed more independence in their voting. But independent of the modification in behaviour, there was a significant structural change. In the 1970s, organizational theory began to have some relevance. The House began to use committees to fulfil specific functions. In seeking to fulfil a scrutinizing role, peers no longer had to be content with the floor of the House.

Committees were not unknown to the Lords before 1970. It already had committees that could be described as being of a 'domestic' nature, concerned for example with the procedure, administration and privileges of the House. It had joint committees with the Commons on consolidation Bills and on statutory instruments. At one time, it even had – like the Commons – standing committees to take the committee stage of Bills. Two such committees were established in 1890 on an experimental basis, but they were abolished in 1910 after complaints were made that they had introduced amendments of substance to the Bills referred to them.[1] (It also had committees to deal with private legislation, with which we are not concerned.) Nonetheless, prior to 1970, the Lords was not in the habit of using committees either for the scrutiny of legislation or for particular sectors of government responsibility. Bills were normally taken in Committee of the Whole House. There were no committees equivalent to the select committees that were being experimented with in the House of Commons. The position was to change markedly in the 1970s.

The House has always had the power to appoint select committees *ad hoc* to consider the implication of Bills presented to it. Rarely has it been thought necessary to use such power in dealing with public general legislation.[2] Since 1976, however, these *ad hoc* committees have formed a much greater part of the Lords' work and have helped to improve the reputation of the House significantly. There has been at least one such committee appointed per session since 1976 and the reports of some have had a direct effect on public legislation. Subjects covered have ranged from hare coursing to small charities, from sexual discrimination to commodity prices. The most recent example is the Select Committee on Overseas Trade, appointed in July 1984. These committees have been notable for their dedication in meeting and in taking evidence. The Committee on Laboratory Animals Protection, for example, met on 16 occasions and in response to its invitation for comments from members of the public and interested bodies received some 900 letters and memoranda. Similarly, the Committee on Foreign Boycotts met 18 times, taking evidence in a written and/or oral form from a total of 57 sources, while the Committee on Commodity Prices met a total of 48 times over the course of two sessions. According to one source, it is not the number of such committees which have been important, but the fact that they have been very productive in raising issues and helping to concentrate the minds of all those involved in the legislative process.[3] Perhaps the most notable example occurred in May 1977 when, following the Second Reading debate on a Bill of Rights introduced by Lord Wade, the House appointed a select committee 'to consider whether a Bill of Rights is desirable and, if so, what form it should take'. In a thorough report, the committee detailed the arguments for and against such a Bill and in so doing contributed much to the wider debate then taking place on the subject.[4]

However, it is in the other sphere of scrutiny, not covering the formal legislative process, that the House has experimented most extensively – and most dramatically – with committees. By 1980, the House could claim effective use of committees for scrutiny of various sectors of public policy; and its most significant committee had a reputation for being not only highly and widely respected, but also for being much more effective than its Commons' counterpart.

In the past decade, the House has appointed committees to undertake scrutinizing functions in three distinct areas: science and technology, unemployment, and European Communities legislation.

Of these, the two most recent have been those on unemployment and science and technology. The committees on science and technology and on EC legislation were appointed on a sessional (i.e. regular) basis; that on unemployment was appointed – like other *ad hoc* committees – for the purpose of undertaking one particular enquiry. The effect of all three may well be to encourage the creation of further such committees in future years.

The Select Committee on Unemployment was appointed in November 1979 to 'consider and make recommendations on long-term remedies for unemployment'. It differed from other *ad hoc* committees in terms of the length of its service and the depth of its enquiries. It comprised 12 members, including businessmen, academics, former MPs, an author and a bishop. Among the politicians, two were former Cabinet ministers, one of whom (though a rare attender at meetings) had been Secretary of State for Employment. The committee's 205-page report was two-and-a-half years in the making. During that time the committee collected evidence from 68 sources. Witnesses included six government departments, the Trades Union Congress, the Confederation of British Industry, the Manpower Services Commission, academics, MPs and a host of corporations, federations and associations. In addition, the committee studied numerous papers and publications in the literature on unemployment from these and other sources.

It is evident from speeches made during a subsequent debate on unemployment in the Commons – in July 1982 – that the report had been read by many of the speakers, including ministers, its recommendations forming the basis of the motion on which the debate took place. Opening the debate, Liberal spokesman David Penhaligon described the report as 'a remarkably useful document. If I could make the report compulsory reading for nearly all honourable Members, I would achieve something useful.'[5] Replying to the debate, the Minister of State for Employment, Michael Alison, referred to the committee's report at differing times as stimulating, interesting and constructive. While he felt the Lords' proposals went beyond the limit of what the government was prepared to accept (involving, on the government's estimate, an extra £5 billion on the total level of public expenditure), he nonetheless emphasized that the government would not be ruling out any of the committee's ideas and that 'the matter has caught our eye and we shall do our best to respond constructively.'[6]

In December 1979, the Lords approved a recommendation from their own Procedure Committee to appoint a Select Committee on Science and Technology. The committee took over the work previously carried out by the House of Commons' Committee in this field. (The Commons' committee was abolished earlier in 1979, after 13 years in existence, following the introduction of a new system of select committees – see chapter 3.) The committee reports on subjects of its own choosing and enquiries are carried out by two sub-committees, each comprising half the committee's membership. The committee has the power to co-opt Lords to the sub-committees for specific enquiries and may (and in practice does) also enlist the services of specialist advisers. The committee produces an average of two reports each session. These reports are usually full and detailed in scope; indeed, one of the criticisms of the committee is that its reports are so detailed that it has been difficult for anyone, other than an expert, to understand them.

The Lords' committee is arguably better equipped to carry out effective scrutiny in this area than was the previous committee in the Commons. The power to co-opt members has allowed the committee to draw upon Lords with considerable practical knowledge in the fields of science and technology. At its inception there were already a hundred peers who were members of the unofficial Parliamentary and Scientific Committee and 13 Fellows of the Royal Society. These, together with a number of scientists, engineers, physicists, biologists and chemists (many more than are found in the Commons) have enabled the Lords' committee to become a highly regarded and 'significant successor to the earlier Commons one'.[7] A report published in December 1980, for example, on the 'Scientific Aspects of Forestry' received the following government response:

The Government welcome the detailed and comprehensive report . . . by the Lordships Select Committee. . . . The choice of the subject for study was opportune at a time when the Government were considering their general policy towards forestry, and the Select Committee's Report makes a valuable contribution towards our thinking on the organisation and co-ordination of the forestry research that will be required to further the policies announced in the Statement made to your Lordships.[8]

Committees have clearly added a new dimension to the workings of the House of Lords. The most significant, however – and the one with the greatest impact – has undoubtedly been the committee set up to deal with European Communities proposals. Anyone walking down the committee corridors, or browsing through the Sessional Papers of the House of Lords, cannot fail to be struck by the emphasis given to work involving the European Communities. Those who dig a little deeper, as we have, will be further struck by the dedicated and enterprising manner in which the House of Lords has tackled the scrutiny of legislative instruments emanating from Brussels.

The work of the Lords in this field is central to any discussion concerning structural changes in the second chamber over the past decade. For this reason we now propose to look in some depth at the EC Committee and in particular at three questions: How did it evolve? How does it operate? And with what effect?

The Select Committee on the European Communities

Creation

The United Kingdom's accession to the European Community in January 1973, following the passage of the European Communities Act of 1972, was one of the major and most contentious legislative events of the modern period and one which has had far-reaching consequences for all British institutions.

Under the Treaty of Rome of 1957, all member states of the European Community are subject to legislation agreed to by the institutions of the Community. Parliament under the 1972 Act has provided that the rights and obligations stemming from this European legislation 'shall be recognised and available in this country, and will be enforced, allowed and followed accordingly'.

Acceding to the Community, then, has been of fundamental legal and institutional significance to the UK. The traditional sovereignty of Parliament rests on the fact that the executive cannot legislate without the consent of Parliament. Membership of the EC weakens this principle since the participation of government in Community law-making is, over a wide range of policy issues, beyond the reach of Parliament. Although Parliament may be called upon on occasion to give its approval to certain measures affecting the constitutional basis of the Community, and is ultimately supreme in that it could repeal the 1972 Act, the fact remains that Community legislation, in the fields covered by the treaties, takes precedence over national law in the UK, and in the case of conflict with national law, Community law prevails. The effect of Britain's membership of the EC has been, as Frank Gregory notes, 'to add a range of new problems to a legislature that already felt itself to be staggering under the pressure of domestic legislation and executive domination'.[9]

Although under the basic treaties establishing the Communities, no official role is given to national legislatures in the enactment of Community measures, there is nothing to prevent national parliaments from developing their own procedures in order to gain a degree of influence over Community proposals. In the UK, the most serious initial problem was the lack of any procedures for the systematic scrutiny of legislative proposals and other Commission documents. In the first full year of membership, a total of 252 regulations, having been approved by the Council of Ministers, took effect in the UK without having received any form of parliamentary scrutiny.

The first stage was the setting up of two *ad hoc* committees in Parliament to examine the question of scrutinizing pre-legislative proposals. (The aim of both Houses was to enter the Community legislative process at an early stage by seeking to influence the government's representatives on the Council of Ministers.) The committees, under the chairmanship of Lord Maybray-King in the Lords and Sir John Foster in the Commons, began work immediately.

The Maybray-King Committee ignored government advice that a standing committee would be the most appropriate means for scrutinizing EC secondary legislation, and instead recommended, in its first report, that a joint select committee of both Houses be set up to sift proposals. The suggestion was not endorsed by the Foster Committee, due to what it saw as being the differing political role and make-up of the two Houses, and was eventually rejected. Thereafter the scrutiny procedures in the two Houses evolved in completely different ways.

After having taken evidence in several other member states the Maybray-King Committee produced its second and major report in July 1973. The report was warmly received when it was debated in the House in December; and the scrutiny procedure in the Lords closely follows its recommendations. It was not until May 1974 however – some 16 months after accession – that the committee's chief recommendation was realized when the House of Lords Select Committee on the European Communities was eventually appointed with the following terms of reference:

To consider Community proposals whether in draft or otherwise, to obtain all necessary information about them, and to make reports on those which, in the opinion of the Committee, raise important questions of policy or principle, and on other questions to which the Committee consider that the special attention of the House should be drawn.

Operation

The Lords' committee now comprises 24 members who meet on a fortnightly basis when the House is sitting. The members of the committee, like most select committees of the House,[10] are selected and proposed to the House by the Lords' Committee of Selection. At the beginning of each session, the chairman is appointed by the House to the salaried position of Principal Deputy Chairman of Committees.

Due to the vast number of proposals and other documents emanating from the Commission, the chairman of the committee, aided by an explanatory memorandum issued by the appropriate government department, conducts an initial sift, setting aside approximately one-quarter which he or she considers worthy of further consideration.[11] The proposals are then listed in the Committee's fortnightly Progress of Scrutiny Report. List A contains the less important proposals thought not to require further attention. List B proposals – those which do require special scrutiny – are then further divided into those 'for detailed consideration' and those for which the chairman would like more information before coming to a decision. Although members of the committee are free to query the categorization of proposals, in practice the chairman's decision is rarely questioned. Nonetheless, dealing with so many proposals, the chairman may on occasion miss the significance of a document.[12]

The Maybray-King Committee originally estimated that around 5 per cent of proposals would be remitted under List B. The figure, however, has been considerably higher. Between March 1983 and March 1984, 25 per cent of all proposals received (197 out of a total of 788) were in fact sent for further consideration.

The role of the chairman in this process is, quite clearly, central. The committee to date has had five chairmen (Lord Diamond; Baroness Tweedsmuir of Belhelvie; Lord Greenwood of Rossendale; Baroness White; and the current chairman, Baroness Llewelyn-Davies of Hastoe). In addition to carrying the burden of 'the sift', the chairman plays a key role in the selection of committee members and in the appointment of sub-committee chairmen.[13] Indeed, the role of the chairman has been described as being akin to that of the whole EC Committee in the Commons.

The task of giving EC proposals adequate scrutiny is, nonetheless, quite clearly beyond the capabilities of one individual, and indeed beyond the capacity of the full committee. The committee has therefore made wide use of its power to appoint specialist sub-committees. The committee may refer to the sub-committees any of the matters within the terms of reference of the committee itself. There are currently seven such sub-committees in operation: these are listed in table 6.1. Of these, six are responsible for considering Community proposals and documents within particular policy areas,

*Table 6.1   House of Lords Select Committee on European Communities:
sub-committees, 1983/4 session*

Sub-committee	Chairman
A Finance, Economics and Regional Policy	Lord O'Brien of Lothbury (life peer; Independent)
B External Relations, Trade and Industry	Lord Brimelow (life peer; Labour)
C Education, Employment and Social Affairs	Lord Seebohm (life peer; Independent)
D Agriculture and Consumer Affairs	Lord Plowden (life peer; Independent)
E Law	Lord Templeman (law lord)
F Energy, Transport, Technology and Research	Lord Kings Norton (life peer; Independent)
G Environment	Lord Nathan (hereditary peer; Independent)

whilst one, Sub-committee E, considers the legal implications of every proposal. This is often done in conjunction with another sub-committee – the Draft Regulation on the European Development Fund, for example, was considered by Sub-committee E together with Sub-committee A (Finance, Economics and Regional Policy).

Each sub-committee has from two to four members; most members of the main committee serve on at least one of the sub-committees. In addition, the main committee may co-opt other lords as members of the sub-committees. There are currently 72 lords co-opted, bringing the total number of peers actively involved in the scrutiny of EC proposals to 96 (this compares with only 16 MPs actively involved in the House of Commons). The ability to co-opt members has enabled the committee to bring into the arena peers with special knowledge and experience in particular areas of EC legislation. In addition, under the terms of Standing Order No. 62 (all lords may attend and speak but not vote), lords with a specific interest or expertise may attend meetings of the select committee and its sub-committees at which instruments on that subject are being discussed. The committee publishes and circulates a weekly broadsheet with a view to keeping other members of the House and the public fully informed of committee agenda and meetings and, as far as possible, with minutes of proceedings.

The procedure followed by the sub-committees is invariably similar to that adopted by the main committee. Commission proposals are published when they are submitted to the Council of Ministers. The government has undertaken to make copies of such proposals available to both Houses of Parliament as soon as is possible, usually within two working days. The appropriate government department then prepares an explanatory memorandum, summarizing the proposals and indicating its legal and policy implications, and the likely timetable of its consideration by the Council. The memorandum is then signed by the relevant minister and submitted to Parliament, usually within a fortnight of the proposal's publication. An average of 66 proposals are deposited each month with the select committee.

It is at this point that the sifting process mentioned earlier takes place, with the most important proposals going to the relevant sub-committee for consideration. Often the sub-committee will take note of the proposal but decide not to give it any further attention. Less than one-tenth of the proposals are the subjects of reports of the House. Of these, less than half are reported as being suitable for debate.

Sub-committee reports are based on evidence collected from a number of sources. The clerk to the committee will usually start by writing to those bodies likely to be affected by the proposal, requesting written evidence. Having read the evidence, the committee will then decide – time permitting – whether it wishes to call for oral evidence. The weekly broadsheet enables any other individuals or interested bodies to volunteer advice which may be of assistance to the committee. Evidence from government departments is invariably given by officials rather than ministers. Committees restrict themselves to calling for ministers to give evidence only on major occasions.

Having collected sufficient evidence, a draft report outlining the findings and opinions of the committee together with recommendations for future action is drawn up. This is usually done by the clerk or chairman of the committee, or sometimes by the two in consultation; alternatively, and especially when the report is of a complex technical nature, one of the committee's specialist advisers may be responsible for drafting the report. The draft report is then usually sent to the relevant government department for consideration and comment on matters of fact. Any revisions necessary to the report are then made before it is sent to the main committee for a final and careful examination. Although empowered to make any amendments as it sees fit, in the majority of cases the committee will adopt the report as presented by the sub-committee. The committee will then recommend either that the report be for the information of the House or that the House should debate it.

Of the 90 reports submitted by the main committee between January 1980 and April 1984, a total of 65 were recommended for debate. In addition, seven of those intended for the information of the House only were debated when a member of the House used his power to draw to the attention of the House, either by motion or by question, a report he considered worthy of debate.[14] Debate in the House usually takes place on a motion to 'take note' of the report in question; around 4 per cent of the time of the House is devoted to debating EC Committee reports.

Links with the European Parliament. The introduction of direct elections to the European Parliament in 1979 effectively severed the main institutional link that existed between the Westminster and Strasbourg Parliaments. The dual mandate provided, as David Coombes notes, 'an additional means for Parliament at Westminster to influence and control Community business'.[15] Previously, 36 members of the UK Parliament, including peers, were designated members of the European Parliament (MEPs). These members were able directly to relay the events at Strasbourg to their colleagues at Westminster. Today, only three peers (all Conservative) – representing in a party capacity specific constituencies, as opposed to representing the national Parliament – serve in the assembly.

Direct elections have not, however, prevented the House of Lords from establishing good informal links with the European Parliament. Members of the Lords' committee occasionally travel to Strasbourg in the course of their enquiries to meet MEPs of all nationalities. A House of Lords' clerk, present at most of the European Parliament's plenary sessions, keeps members of the committee up to date with all major events. Contact is further enhanced by a regular flow of paper in both directions between the committees of the Lords and the European Parliament.

Effect

In order to assess the effectiveness of the Lords' committee, it may serve as a useful exercise to start by drawing some comparisons with the committee's counterpart in the House of Commons. The Select Committee on European Legislation was established in May 1974 following the recommendations of the Foster Committee. Although on the face of it appointed along much the same lines as the Lords' committee, there are essential differences between the two.

The major function of the 16-strong Commons committee is to consider draft proposals emanating from the Commission, and to recommend to the House for further consideration those proposals that, in their opinion, raise questions of legal and political importance. Unlike in the Lords, there is no sifting process by the chairman; every proposal is considered by the committee. And it is the job of the House as a whole, not the committee, to pronounce on the merits and substance of Commission proposals submitted to the Council of Ministers. The Commons' committee is, therefore, essentially a political filter whose main task, as one commentator observes, is 'to sort out wheat from chaff on the Commons behalf'.[16]

The importance of the committee's work is based on an undertaking given by the government to both Houses in 1974 that ministers would not, except in matters of urgency, consent in the Council of Ministers to any proposal if it still awaited recommended debate in either House. When asked to give such an undertaking, Roy Hattersley, then Minister for Foreign and Commonwealth Affairs and responsible for keeping Parliament informed of all EC proposals, told the House: 'Certainly. In the case of legislative instruments any other arrangement would be intolerable.'[17]

Despite this undertaking, however, the Commons committee has faced a number of problems. If the committee alerts the attention of the House to a proposal, it may be debated either on the floor of the House or, since 1975, in standing committee. Objection is frequently raised, however, to any proposed reference to standing committee. This is due in part to the continuing political controversy that surrounds Britain's membership of the EC. As a result, it is not uncommon for debates on EC proposals to take place in the House late at night when the few members who attend repeatedly find themselves discussing matters of far more detail and complexity than they were used to before the UK's accession.[18] Moreover, the timetable of the House is already congested, with little enough time for domestic legislation; great difficulties have therefore been experienced in arranging debates, recommended by the committee, in time for the House to express its views on a proposal before a decision is taken in the Council of Ministers. In the case of fast-moving proposals, the ability of members to exercise any real influence over the minister's mandate is clearly restricted, and has led one study group to conclude that 'The traditional domination of Parliamentary proceedings by the government's business managers has continued.'[19]

The delay in considering reports, together with the restrictive terms of reference and the lack of any formal power, has reduced the effectiveness of the committee and led one member of the Lords' committee to remark that the scrutiny system in the Commons is nothing more than 'an early-warning system for the House as a whole and could be done by one good journalist. The whole thing is a self-defeating exercise because of the obsession with the "floor of the House" supremacy.'[20]

In order to prevent the unnecessary duplication of work, the EC committees of the two Houses have, since December 1975, had the power to 'confer and meet concurrently.' The committees, through their respective sub-committees, have used this power to hear evidence and deliberate together whilst still producing separate reports. The nature of the two systems means nonetheless that there is little overlap between the Lords and the Commons. The lords who took part in a study undertaken in 1984 by David Morton admitted to meeting rarely, either formally or informally, with members of the Commons' committee. On the whole, it would seem that the concurrent meetings have not proved a great success. Nevertheless, contact and co-operation between the two Houses is maintained, generally by the informal exchange of papers and by liaison between the clerks and other staff.

The Lords, it would seem, leave the Commons to deal with fast-moving, highly political issues by debate on the floor, while they concentrate on 'the no less essential and informative role of dealing in a more detached and thorough way with the wider legal and administrative measures'.[21] This division of labour, Coombes suggests, 'might be regarded as appropriate to the differences in functions of the two chambers'.[22]

The Lords' committee clearly does possess a number of considerable advantages over its counterpart in the Commons, and is generally considered to have made the more positive contribution to Westminster's scrutiny. In the Lords, the timetable is less rigid, the party divide less apparent and the membership often professionally expert in the subject under review. The Lords' committees are able to take evidence and operate in an atmosphere less abrasive than that which characterizes proceedings in the Commons. With less restrictive terms of reference and greater time and manpower resources at their disposal, the Lords' committees have been able to consider proposals in far greater depth and scope than is possible in the Commons. Indeed a report published in 1977 by an independent working party sponsored by the Hansard Society, on the effects of membership of the EC on representative institutions stated: 'we are struck by the relevance and businesslike nature of the results of the Lords' work in this field, and think it significant that the Commons, who are meant to represent the people of this country, have taken in contrast to the Lords a largely inward-looking and conservative attitude where the opposite was required.'[23]

A study by David Brew, published in 1979, revealed that on the whole scrutineers in the Lords thought they were doing a better job than the Commons, with 10 out of 11 believing the scrutiny system in the Lords operated 'satisfactorily' (compared with 9 out of 14 MPs who were dissatisfied with the procedures for scrutiny in the Commons). The general feeling as far as the House of Lords was concerned was that 'a useful job was being done very efficiently and there was little scope for improvement.'[24]

Evidence suggests that the reports produced by the Lords' committee have been widely read and highly regarded by all concerned. The chairman of the Commons European Committee, Nigel Spearing, recently described the Lords' reports as 'voluminous and very full in their coverage', whilst a spokesman from the Department of Trade and Industry admitted to finding them 'very useful' and often to recommending them as a reference work to interested bodies.[25] The reports are also appreciated by many outside Westminster and Whitehall. One MEP told Morton that he found the reports 'extremely helpful' while serving on the Assembly's Economic and Monetary Committee; and David Lea, assistant general secretary of the TUC, has written: 'Maybe we [the TUC] ought to think about how one would differentiate the useful enquiries from the rest. We find the House of Lords select committee work on European Community matters quite useful, because at the end of the day they do tell us quite a lot about the purposes of some European proposals, more clearly than the Commission itself.'[26] The ability of the Lords to examine rather than simply identify important issues has allowed them to address their reports to a wide audience.[27]

The 21 reports published by the committee in the 1981/2 session (see table 6.2) illustrate the range and diversity of its work. They included reports on 'The Borrowing and Lending Activities of the EC' and 'Noise in the Environment'; on 'Agricultural Trade Policy' and 'Beverage Containers'. The committee's most recent report 'Youth Training in the EEC', published in August 1984, took nine months to prepare after evidence was collected in almost every other EEC country, as well as from some UK government departments and numerous interested organizations and individuals.

A report published in 1982 by a study group of the Commonwealth Parliamentary Association found the Lords' reports to contain 'the

Table 6.2 House of Lords Select Committee on the European Communities: reports and evidence, 1981/2 session

Total number of reports issued by the main committee		21
Reports emanating from sub-committees	A	4
	B	2
	C	4
	D	3
	E	1
	F	4
	G	3
	Total	21
Total number of pages of reports		318
Average number of pages per report		18
Evidence received	Oral (only)	43
	Written (only)	168
	Oral and written	112
	Total	323
Total number of pages of minutes of evidence		2,519[a]
Average number of pages per report		109

[a]Includes minutes of evidence collected by two sub-committees (B and F) without reports.

only really deep analysis of the issues that is available to the parliamentary representative of the ten countries in the Community.' The report continues:

The Lords' reports are far more informative and comprehensive than those produced by the Commons committee on European legislation. That is because the Lords' committee Members are more objective and often have close knowledge of the subject under scrutiny. In the Commons, party allegiances can come to the fore. The Lords are free to give their frank opinion, and sometimes, it is devastating.[28]

There can be little doubt that the Lords' committee has provided an invaluable parliamentary service in bringing to the attention of all those concerned with the effects of EC legislation its well-researched and highly regarded opinions. The question remains, however, as to whether the work of the Lords in this field has any impact upon the actions of the government in the EC decision-making process. The very nature of that system, as we shall see, means that the influence of Parliament can only ever be limited and indirect. Nevertheless, information and debates arising from the committee's reports do impose some discipline of explanation on the executive. Morton's questionnaire revealed that the general opinion of the Lords was that their reports were 'reasonably influential' and that they had a good effect in concentrating the minds of ministers and providing useful background material for decision-makers.[29] In evidence to the Lords' Committee on Practice and Procedure in 1977, Lady Tweedsmuir contended that, while not necessarily directly affecting legislation, the force of the reports' arguments had on occasion been conceded by government. 'It has been said to us privately, for example, "Oh, we had not thought of that", but it is not the kind of thing that one could publish or say openly on the floor of the House.'[30]

Indeed, in some respects, EC membership has opened up a chink for the Lords to exploit. Previously, for example, the general debate in both Houses on the government's annual White Paper on Agriculture did not allow for any real cross-examining of government proposals and invariably produced little change. The Lords' committee, through its sub-committee on agriculture, has provided now an opportunity for detailed questioning of policy in this area.

As well as prelegislative scrutiny, the Lords' committee has also on occasion brought to the attention of the government the consequences of enacted legislation. In the 1974/5 session the committee's 33rd report drew attention to the Measurement of Cereals for Import and Export Purposes Regulations which transpired to be *ultra vires*. The report, and the following debate, revealed a serious deficiency in the parliamentary scrutiny process of European legislation. The Lord Chancellor promptly agreed to amend by subsequent statutory instrument the offending instrument and drew attention to the 'valuable illustration of the role of the Committees which are set up in maintaining the oversight, the control, of Parliament over this aspect of Directives emanating from Brussels'.[31]

So far the success of the House of Lords' committee has been emphasized, but it is not without its serious limitations. Procedural obstacles include the fact that whilst finding time for recommended debates is not a serious problem, difficulties do arise over the erratic nature of the Council of Ministers' agenda. The speed at which EC decisions are made varies considerably: 'Some proposals are extremely fast moving and are adopted within a few days; others may take years.'[32] It is also difficult to foretell the amount of time that will be taken over the preparation of a proposal – a forecast on which the scrutiny committees must prepare their work. The Annual Budget, for example, has a timetable which at present makes it very difficult for the UK Parliament to consider the published proposals (ie. for the committees to report on them and for the House to debate them) before they are considered in the Council of Ministers. Other difficulties, affecting the punctual supply of information, adequate translations of European documents, and the timing of the major EEC instruments, occur from time to time.

In the final analysis, perhaps the most laconic description of the work of the Lords' committee has been provided by Philip Norton, who sees their role as being essentially an 'informative and educative' one. But what precludes it from doing more and having any tangible impact upon the government?

The major problem that the Lords' committee faces is that its role is an advisory one; as a committee of the second chamber it has no sanctions over the passage of EC legislation. Moreover, the committee – and this applies to all Lords' committees – is just one of many bodies of influence whose proposals the government may consider. Often pressure from Commons' backbenchers or powerful interest groups such as the CBI or TUC will carry as much, and usually more, weight. As Brew's study illustrates, the influence of the Lords' is by its very nature limited; at the end of the day it is the Commons which exercises the 'necessary political punch' with the Lords committee providing 'some of the ammunition'.[33] It is significant, for example, that in Gregory's study of major EC policy areas from a British perspective, little reference is made to the House of Lords.[34]

The authority of the Lords' committee reports derives from who is on the committee rather than what the committee is. In other words, it is the committee's status as a highly regarded and professionally expert body working diligently to produce complete and informative reports in a less partisan atmosphere, which enables it to wield some influence, rather than its status as a committee of the House of Lords, which affords little political clout *per se*.

Conclusion

The use of committees has helped to inject a new lease of life into a House that was somewhat indifferent, even with regard to its own future, as late as the 1960s. All the indications are that since that time committees have made a modest but nonetheless significant contribution in specific areas to the parliamentary scrutiny of the executive in the UK. As Donald Shell has written: 'It is easy to criticise the role of select committees, and hard to give convincing answers to searching questions about their effectiveness, but the point can be made that the Lords has through such committees mobilised considerable expertise at virtually no expense to investigate and report on subjects which have been of some parliamentary concern.'[35]

The success of those committees already in operation may well provide the impetus needed for the creation of other scrutiny committees in the future. Lord Denham, government chief whip in the Lords, for one, believes the development of the EC Committee will lead eventually to a network of domestic scrutiny committees being set up in the Lords.[36] The EC Committee itself has expressed its support for a series of such committees.[37]

But what provided the impetus for the changes which have already taken place? The answer as far as the EC Committee is concerned may be given in terms of the confluence of EC membership, which generated the need for structural change, and the attitudinal and behavioural changes that were taking place at the same time and for the reasons outlined in the preceding chapter.

Select committees have provided one channel through which the new professionalism and greater independence of the House have been expressed. The most important factor contributing to the change has been the infusion of life peers following the Life Peerages Act 1958. Table 6.3 highlights this and supports the arguments advanced by Baldwin. The proportion of hereditary peers to life peers in the

Table 6.3 Number of life and hereditary peers serving on EC Committees during 1981/2 session

	Peers serving on main committee	Peers serving on sub-committees (members plus co-opted members)							
		A	B	C	D	E	F	G	Total
Life	15	11	9	13	8	10	9	5	80
Hereditary	8	5	5	1	5	1	6	6	37
Total	23								117

Table 6.4 Party breakdown of peers involved in the scrutiny of EC legislation, 1981/2 session

| | Peers serving on main committee | Peers serving on sub-committees (members plus co-opted members) | | | | | | | |
		A	B	C	D	E	F	G	Total
Conservative	8	3	4	4	4[a]	3	5	5	36
Labour	5	4	3	1	4	3	2	1	23
Liberal	2	–	3	2	1	1	1	1	11
SDP	1	1	1	1	3	–	1	1	9
Independent	5	4	1	3	1	–	5	2	21
Crossbenchers	–	2	–	3	–	–	–	–	5
No party declared	2	2	2	–	–	4	1	1	12
Total	23								117

[a]Includes one Ulster Unionist.

House as a whole is 7:3, and among the 300 or so active members of the House the proportion is 5:5.[38] However, the proportion of those serving on the select committee and its sub-committees (members plus co-opted members) in 1981/2 was 3:7, the exact reverse of the proportion of hereditary to life peers among the total membership. Furthermore, the current chairman of the committee and six out of seven sub-committee chairmen are life peers.

Membership of the European Communities and the influx of life peers thus provide the basis for the creation of the EC Committee. Two further factors have facilitated the effectiveness of the committee. One is the absence of a party majority (table 6.4). In the selection of members, specialist knowledge is a more important criterion than party affiliation.[39] While the proportion of Conservatives to non-Conservatives in the House as a whole is 5:5, and among the active membership 4:6, of those involved in the scrutiny of EC legislation the proportion is 3:7. As table 6.4 demonstrates, though there may be a plurality of Conservative members involved in the committee work, there is nothing remotely resembling a majority. Indeed, the current chairman of the committee, Baroness Llewelyn-Davies of Hastoe is a Labour member and a former government chief whip; and of the seven sub-committee chairmen, five are Independents, one Labour and one a law lord. Given that no one party enjoys a majority in either the full committee or any one of the sub-committees, appeals to partisan loyalty are of little use. Even more than on the floor of the House, the EC Committee and its sub-committees avoid the adversary conflict that characterizes behaviour in the House of Commons. Consequently, votes are rare.[40]

The second factor is that the committee harbours no significant number of peers opposed to Britain's membership of the European Communities. That this should be so is not surprising, reflecting as it does the preponderant support within the House itself for British membership. In the Lords, the 1972 European Communities Bill did not prove to be the contentious measure that it had been in the Commons. (In 1971, their lordships had approved the principle of entry by 451 votes to 58.) As a result, the committee is able to avoid both a party and a pro-EC/anti-EC division, freeing it to concentrate upon the scrutinizing role ascribed to it by the House and to reach, in the words of Sir John Eden, 'dispassionate conclusions on Community matters'.[41] In short, the committee has members able and willing to serve and is free of the encumbrances that are features of its Commons' counterpart.

The House of Lords suffers from being 'unrepresentative' and its authority from being less 'legitimate' than that of the elected House of Commons. There is no way that it can enjoy the political clout of the lower House. It constitutes but a minor influence amongst a welter of more powerful groups seeking to influence government. Yet the behavioural changes described in chapter 5, which have manifested themselves in the structural changes here outlined, have helped to increase the respect in which the House is held and have enabled the Lords to exert a degree of influence. The role of the EC Committee is essentially an informative and educative one – there is little else it could be given the nature of the House – but it is a role that it fulfils well, at little cost and to the benefit of all interested parties. Short of major reform of the House of Lords, it is difficult to see how the authority of the committee could be enhanced. Yet reform of the Lords could rob the committee of those very characteristics which at the moment make for its effectiveness. For the committee to resemble its Commons' counterpart would be a negative, not a positive, step.

Notes

The idea for this chapter derives from an original dissertation on the Lords' European Communities Committee by Caroline Moore (now Mrs Caroline

Moore Hodgson), completed in Hull University Politics Department in 1979; the updating, additional research and writing of the chapter has been undertaken by Cliff Grantham.

1 P. Bromhead, *The House of Lords and Contemporary Politics 1911–1957* (London: Routledge & Kegan Paul, 1958), p. 131.

2 Hybrid Bills, not the focus of our concern here, are normally referred to select committees. On hybrid Bills, see P. Norton, *The Commons in Perspective* (Oxford: Martin Robertson, 1981), p. 104.

3 Official in the House of Lords, to Cliff Grantham, interview, 1984.

4 See P. Norton, *The Constitution in Flux* (Oxford: Martin Robertson, 1982), p. 246, and the report itself: House of Lords Select Committee on a Bill of Rights, *Report*, HL 176.

5 *HC Deb.* 27, col. 66.

6 *HC Deb.* 27, col. 106.

7 P. Bromhead and D. Shell, 'The British Constitution in 1970', *Parliamentary Affairs*, 33(2), 1980, p. 151.

8 HL Sessional Papers 1981/2, vol. XIII.

9 F.E.C. Gregory, *Dilemmas of Government: Britain and the European Community* (Oxford: Martin Robertson, 1983), p. 122.

10 There are exceptions: the Committee of Selection itself, judicial committees, the Joint Committee on Consolidation Bills and the Ecclesiastical Committee do not have their members nominated by the Committee of Selection.

11 On the sifting process, see the evidence of Baroness Tweedsmuir to the House of Lords Select Committee on Procedure and Practice, *Minutes of Evidence*, HL 141 (London: HMSO, 1977), pp. 52–3.

12 Lady Tweedsmuir recalled one occasion when the chairman of Sub-committee B (Lord Selkirk) drew to her attention an important document on hallmarking which she had put on List A. 'I missed it because I did not realise its significance at the time. He was quite right': ibid., p. 45

13 See ibid., p. 46.

14 D. Morton, 'The Role of the House of Lords in the Scrutiny of EEC Legislation' (third-year undergraduate dissertation, Hull University Politics Department, 1984).

15 D. Coombes, 'Parliament and the European Community', in S.A. Walkland and M. Ryle (eds), *The Commons Today* (London: Fontana, 1981), p. 243.

16 E. Taylor, *The House of Commons at Work*, 9th edition (London: Macmillan, 1979), p. 176.

17 *HC Deb.* 874, col. 1547.

18 Taylor, *The House of Commons at Work*, p. 175.

19 C. Sasse, E. Poullet, D. Coombes and G. Deprez, *Decision Making in the European Community* (New York: Praeger, 1977), p. 319.

20 See D. Brew, 'National Parliamentary Scrutiny of European Community Legislation: The Case of the United Kingdom Parliament', in V. Herman

and R. van Schendelen (eds), *The European Parliament and National Parliaments* (Farnborough: Saxon House, 1979), p. 249.

21 The Hansard Society, *The British People: Their Voice in Europe* (Farnborough: Saxon House, 1977), p. 40.

22 Coombes, 'Parliament and the European Community', p. 249.

23 Hansard Society, *The British People*, p. 40.

24 Brew, 'National Parliamentary Scrutiny of European Community Legislation', p. 250.

25 Morton, 'The Role of the House of Lords in the Scrutiny of EEC legislation', p. 26.

26 D. Lea, 'A Trade Unionist's View', in D. Englefield (ed.), *Commons Select Committees: Catalysts for Progress?* (London: Longman, 1984), p. 53.

27 An example given by Gregory is the Lords' European Committee report, 'European Institutions (Three Wise Men) and the Spierenburg Report', on the organization and working of the EC. Gregory, *Dilemmas of Government*, p. 119.

28 The Report of a Study Group of the Commonwealth Parliamentary Association, 'The Role of Second Chambers', *The Parliamentarian*, 63(4), October 1982, p. 207.

29 Morton, 'The Role of the House of Lords in the Scrutiny of EEC legislation', p. 27.

30 Baroness Tweedsmuir, in *Minutes of Evidence*, p. 56.

31 *HL Deb.* 368, cols 413–17.

32 Quoted in Norton, *The Commons in Perspective*, p. 191.

33 Brew, 'National Parliamentary Scrutiny of European Community Legislation', p. 250.

34 Gregory, *Dilemmas of Government*, ch. 6.

35 D. Shell, 'The House of Lords', in D. Judge (ed.), *The Politics of Parliamentary Reform* (London: Heinemann, 1983), p. 102.

36 Talking to a group of students from Hull University Politics Department, 7 March 1984.

37 Memorandum by the European Communities Committee to the House of Lords Select Committee on Practice and Procedure, *Minutes of Evidence*, HL 141 (London: HMSO, 1977), pp. 41–2.

38 Calculated from N. Baldwin, 'The House of Lords: A Study in Evolutionary Adaptability', *Hull Papers in Politics No. 33* (Hull: Hull University Politics Department, 1983), p. 14.

39 See the comments of Lady Tweedsmuir, in *Minutes of Evidence*, p. 52. 'We really look first of all at those who are specialists when we are co-opting, then we realise we are getting unbalanced [party politically] one way and the other and we rush round and try and persuade somebody else to join us to correct this.'

40 In 1977, Lady Tweedsmuir, as chairman of the committee, recorded, 'we have only once had a vote in Committee': Lady Tweedsmuir, ibid., p. 56.

41 Memorandum submitted by Sir John Eden, chairman of the Commons' Select Committee on European Legislation, to the Commons' Select Committee on Procedure, July 1977. *First Report from the Select Committee on Procedure, 1977/78*, vol. II: Minutes of Evidence, HC 588–2 (London: HMSO, 1978), p. 194.

7

Conclusion
Parliamentary Reform: Where To From Here?

Philip Norton

Pressure for parliamentary reform was a feature of the 1960s and the 1970s. There was clearly a felt need for reform. Is there a need for reform in the 1980s?

According to some politicians, the answer is no. Enoch Powell and Michael Foot argued against the reforms of the 1970s, Mr Foot being an ardent opponent of the 1978 Procedure Committee's recommendation in favour of select committees. Both continue to be associated with opposition to significant structural reforms, at least of the House of Commons (Mr Foot supports abolition of the House of Lords). The House of Commons, according to Mr Powell, is constantly and almost imperceptibly changing, sufficient to meet the demands placed upon it.[1] The chamber of the House of Commons is, according to such politicians, the focus of political debate and should remain so. There is no need for extensive change.

In their support, Messrs Powell and Foot would appear able to call upon a significant section of popular opinion. In Almond and Verba's classic study published in 1963, more Britons expressed pride in their governmental and political institutions than in any other feature of the nation that was mentioned.[2] Perceptions of the House of Commons as an effective working body have shown no significant decline since that time. A National Opinion Poll undertaken for Granada Television in 1973 on attitudes towards Parliament failed to detect the degree of dissatisfaction that was expected.[3] Of those questioned, 55 per cent agreed with the statement that 'Parliament works very well or fairly well'; only 8 per cent thought that MPs were doing 'a poor job'. A MORI poll carried out for *The Sunday Times* in 1977 on how well institutions performed found that 'Parliament emerges with surprisingly little egg on its face', only 8 per cent of respondents considering that Parliament did 'a bad job'.[4] Indeed, dissatisfaction with institutions of government showed no great increase in the 1970s, despite what may be expected.[5] Reform of institutions such as the House of Commons or the House of Lords was not accorded any significant priority by citizens.[6]

And, of course, recent years have witnessed the changes detailed in the preceding chapters. The House of Commons has experienced notable behavioural changes, both inside the House (greater voting independence) and outside (pursuit of constituency casework); it has witnessed the most significant structural reform of more than half a century with the creation of the new select committees and it has undergone other noteworthy structural and procedural changes. The House of Lords has witnessed also remarkable behavioural changes: peers are more independent in their voting behaviour, more of them attend the House, and they sit for longer hours. The use of committees, primarily but not exclusively for scrutiny of draft European Communities' legislation, has been a major constitutional departure. As is clear from the preceding chapters, both Houses of Parliament have undergone major changes. Neither is the institution it was in the 1950s and 1960s.

Is there, then, a case for reform? The answer is yes. The reforms detailed above constitute but a partial solution to Parliament's attempts to fulfil more effectively the functions ascribed to it. As I mentioned in chapter 2, cohesion remains a feature of parliamentary behaviour; an extremely large parliamentary majority makes backbench influence more difficult to achieve. Select committees, as Stephen Downs has shown, have made some contribution to greater parliamentary influence, but their role is not well defined and their influence derives from publicity and persuasion; they enjoy no definitive sanctions. In pursuing constituency casework, MPs are fulfilling a micro rather than a macro function. The House of Lords fulfils its functions more effectively than it did before, but it labours under the inherent vulnerability of being an unelected chamber.

There is some notable dissatisfaction with the workings of Parliament (and other political institutions) at an elite level, among some politicians, political writers and, perhaps most notably, university teachers. Academics such as Professor S. A. Walkland have been caustic in their condemnation of Parliament.[7] A new Commons' Reform Group was formed in the new Parliament returned in June 1983, attracting support from all parts of the House. (Its three leaders are Plaid Cymru Member Dafydd Wigley, Conservative William Benyon, and Labour's Austin Mitchell.) A significant fraction of the population also appears disenchanted with the existing political system, reflected in the decline in voter turnout and in the growth of alternative channels of influence to established political institutions (action groups and the like). As we have seen (chapter 1), some groups appear willing to question Parliament's legitimacy to legislate on matters that affect their particular interests.

There is, then, both a *prima facia* case for reform and clearly some pressure for reform. But that pressure is not gathered in one cohesive and structured movement. It takes different forms. Indeed, the approaches can be grouped on the basis of two distinct divisions: (a) there are those that focus on the House of Commons and those that focus on the House of Lords; and (b) there are those that seek to achieve change within the exciting parliamentary framework (in essence, seeking incremental change) and those that seek to achieve radical, transformative reform, external to the structures of the House. On the basis of these two separate divisions, it is possible to construct a four-box matrix (figure 7.1). The reforms advocated are identified within each box. Those approaches which seek change from within (in

Relationship of reform to existing parliamentary framework	Chamber	
	House of Commons	House of Lords
From within (incremental)	Structural/procedural reforms ('internal reform') Attitudinal change ('Norton View')	Structural/procedural reforms Attitudinal change Reformed composition
External (radical, transformative)	Electoral reform Devolution Bill of Rights	Elected second chamber Abolition (unicameralism)
	Comprehensive reform of Parliament	

Figure 7.1   Approaches to parliamentary reform

both chambers) are concerned primarily with the more effective fulfilment of the function of scrutiny and influence. Those that seek a radical transformation look beyond that function and question Parliament's representative capacity to exercise an effective legitimizing function. They seek a more representative Parliament in order to achieve the fulfilment of its functions.

The House of Commons

Changes from within

Calls for procedural change – or more extensive structural reform – are not new to the House of Commons. Such calls, though, have been notable for being far from extensive and for having little impact. Emphasis on the floor of the House as the place for debate, the absence of full-time, professional Members and the mode of representation in Britain (Members being elected to represent geographically delineated constituencies, each encompassing often disparate interests) produced essentially an 'amateur' House.[8] It served government well to maintain that amateur nature. For much of the twentieth century, Members themselves seemed unwilling to contemplate serious internal change. When a Select Committee on Procedure produced the occasional recommendation for procedural change, such recommendations were not countenanced by government. The consequence was a form of procedural inertia.

Only in post-war years, as the failure of the House to fulfil effectively its scrutinizing function became more apparent, did calls for reform become more strident. Even then, not until the 1960s were they to have much impact upon Members or ministers; and the reforms that were undertaken were limited and their impact not much short of marginal.[9] The most significant of the changes among the 'Crossman reforms' of the 1960s was the creation of the select committees on agriculture and on science and technology; the former was a failure, the latter at best a modest success. The 1970s witnessed further changes, notably the creation of the Expenditure Committee and, more significantly, the new departmentally related select comittees in 1979.

Procedural reformers were not daunted by the failure of the reforms of the 1960s. They sought to achieve no radical shift in the relationship between the House and that part of it which formed the government. They sought instead to shore up the ability of the House to fulfil the function of scrutiny and influence. Procedural reforms – or structural changes such as a more extensive committee system – appeared the obvious, necessary and sufficient means of achieving this. If certain reforms failed to achieve their ends, then other internal reforms should be undertaken.[10]

The past two decades have thus witnessed experimentation in parliamentary procedures and internal structures. Politicians, academics and Select Committees on Procedure have recommended various, often specific and disparate reforms. In the 1960s, proposals for reform came from academics such as Bernard Crick and members of the Study of Parliament Group as well as from Members of Parliament, especially on the Labour side of the House. In the 1980s, pressure for internal reform comes most notably (though not exclusively) from MPs. Academics are now most visible in pressing for radical, external reform.

In the House itself, there are three main sources from which recommendations for reform come: (a) Select Committees on Procedure; (b) the All-Party Commons' Reform Group, and (c) individual Members. The House has set up a number of Procedure Committees, at different times, to examine aspects of its procedure. Of these, the most important of recent years has been that which reported in 1978, recomending the creation of a system of select committees.[11] (A similar recommendation was made in the Eleventh Report from the Expenditure Committee in 1977.) More recently, a Select Committee on Procedure (Supply), which reported in 1981, recommended the introduction of a number of Estimates Days and the replacement of Supply Days with 19 Opposition Days; its recommendations were accepted, in modified form, in July 1982. It was also successful in generating a further committee, the Select Committee on Procedure (Finance), to examine the House's financial procedures. In March 1984, the House appointed a new Procedure Committee to consider the procedure on public Bills in standing committees and indeed any matters of procedure in the conduct of public business as it thought fit. It began to receive evidence in the autumn of that year.

Reform groups are not new to the House of Commons and appear to have had some influence in the reform era of the 1960s. The most recent example is that formed in late 1983. Avoiding the mistake of the reform movement of the 1960s, when separate Labour and Conservative groups were created, the group is an all-party one encompassing Members from all parts of the House. Chaired by Dafydd Wigley, the Plaid Cymru Member for Caernarfon, it has attracted about 40 MPs to its meetings. It favours full-time Members and the provision of more extensive facilities, including in constituencies, for MPs. It has also sought to elicit the views of Members generally, administering a questionnaire to all Members in the summer of 1984. The responses – there was a response rate of 50 per cent – demonstrated support for a number of procedural reforms. Most notably, these included automatic timetabling of Bills (72.8 per cent of all respondents in favour), televising select committees (53.9 per cent in favour), televising proceedings in the chamber (51.6 per cent in favour), more research assistance for Members (54.8 per cent in favour), and parliamentary provision of an office and other facilities in Members' constituencies (51.2 per cent in favour). Labour Members tended to be more reform-minded than Conservative Members, especially on the issue of the provision of constituency facilities.[12]

Support for procedural change has also been articulated by individual Members, sometimes in speeches in the House, sometimes in submissions to Procedure Committees and on occasion in books and articles. Evidence to the 1977/8 Procedure Committee and the 1981 Committee on Procedure (Supply) included a variety of reasoned and detailed proposals from a number of Members.[13] Among these were calls for the creation of select committees, an overhaul of the Commons' procedures for financial scrutiny, and – from John Peyton – the recommendation that standing-committee stage for legislation be vested in select committees.[14] Pamphlets and articles advocating change have come from Members such as Sir Edward du Cann on the Conservative side and Bruce George on the Labour side.[15] The latter has recently reiterated the case for internal reform. The House, he contends, can achieve an effective scrutinizing function through procedural reform, notably through the extension of the select-committee system, the greater use of special standing committees and reform of the procedure for financial oversight. And a more 'professional' House can be achieved, he argues, by an increase in staff – in the personal staff (secretarial and research) of Members, in committee staff and advisers, and in the research staff of the Commons' Library (see appendix 2).[16] The reforms of recent years have, in George's view, been significant. They now need to be consolidated.

Pressure for internal reform has thus been, and remains, important. It retains some notable advocates, not least within the House of Commons itself. However, it has been subject to criticism from two distinct sources. On the one hand, it has been criticized as inadequate and even irrelevant by those who now favour radical, external reform. On the other hand, it has been challenged from a more sympathetic source: by what has been termed by its originator (this writer) as 'the Norton View'. This sees internal reform as necessary and relevant, but urges that it be put in a wider political context.

In the 1970s, the reform movement – in as much as it constituted a movement – split, divided between those who were concerned primarily to enhance the capacity of the House to exert scrutiny and influence within the existing parliamentary framework and those who believed that a more radical transformation was needed. The former continued to press for internal reform. The latter, looking at the economic and political upheavals of the 1970s, argued that extensive constitutional change was needed urgently if the House were to maintain its legitimacy as a representative institution; without that legitimacy, tinkering with the structures and procedures of the House was a tiresome irrelevancy.

The Norton View, in contrast, seeks not to challenge the value of internal reform but rather to provide a means for its realization and to place the case for it in a wider political context. According to this view, the reformers of the 1960s and 1970s neglected to consider how their goal was to be achieved. They had argued for procedures designed to subject the government to more effective critical scrutiny. Yet who had they been dependent upon for the initiation of such procedures? The government itself. The Norton View contends that significant structural and procedural reforms are achievable, but only if the political will exists among MPs as a whole to ensure their implementation and sustenance. The House enjoys the power to compel government to concede reforms. That Members might be persuaded to use their political muscle to compel such changes seemed inconceivable in the 1960s. The experience of the 1970s demonstrated that, far from being inconceivable, it was quite possible. The decade, as we have seen, witnessed major behavioural changes in the division lobbies (chapter 2), beginning in a Parliament in which the government had an overall working majority. A majority of Members proved willing to impose their will on occasion on a reluctant government. That exercise of power in the division lobbies had an immediate effect upon legislation and executive actions. It also provided the means for the realization of structural reform.

The growing awareness among Members of what they could achieve provided the impetus for the select-committee reforms of 1979. It was pressure from backbenchers on all sides of the House that forced the then Leader of the House to concede a debate on the 1978 report from the Procedure Committee; it was demands from Members in that debate that forced the minister to concede a vote on the committee's recommendations; and it was pressure from all sides of the House that impelled a reluctant Cabinet to acquiesce in the setting up of the new committees. The committees, in short, were the creation of the House, not of the government. Further pressure from backbenchers resulted in the Government backing down on the issue of MPs' pay, in the passage of the National Audit Act, and in the implementation of other procedural reforms such as Estimates Days (see appendix 1). It was, declared Edward du Cann in the debate on Estimates Days, 'a reforming Parliament'.[17] The experience of the decade demonstrated that Members could impose their will on government on both substantive as well as procedural matters.

The experience of the 1970s thus gave empirical credence to that part of the Norton View which argues that attitudinal change is a prerequisite for effective structural and procedural change. My 'view' does not stop there. It extends further to stipulate that the behavioural and structural changes of recent years can be – and should be – taken further; and that such a development is necessary to maintain an essential balance in the political system between the imperatives of effectiveness and consent.[18]

At times of economic decline and some political instability, the greater is the need for government effectiveness to be maintained; yet with declining resources to meet commitments of public policy, it is more difficult to maintain that effectiveness. Concomitantly, the challenges faced by government in responding to disparate demands at a time of declining resources increase the need to maintain consent for the institutions and processes of government. Declining support can undermine the effectiveness of government. Hence the necessity to maintain both effectiveness and consent.

Behavioural and structural changes in the House of Commons can contribute to the maintenance of consent without jeopardizing the effectiveness of government. By generating effective means of scrutiny and by being willing to display a degree of independence in their behaviour, Members of Parliament not only can fulfil more effectively the function of scrutiny and influence but at the same time, by being seen to do that which is expected of them, can enhance popular support for the system of government. In so doing, they can provide the broad limits within which government can govern without unduly jeopardizing government effectiveness. Parliament would not become part of the policy-making process; it would not rob the government of its ability to plan a coherent programme, planning within the broad constraint of anticipated parliamentary reaction. In short, government could govern, while the Commons could subject government to effective, and public, scrutiny. The problem with radical, transformative reforms of the House, as we shall see, is that they could undermine government effectiveness and in consequence jeopardize the consent that the reformers crave. Leaving things as they are is not an adequate solution; but major reform external to the existing parliamentary framework is inherently dangerous. Further significant structural and procedural reform is necessary. The impetus for it must come from within the House itself.

External reforms

For many reformers, reforms internal to the House are no longer sufficient. These reformers are not necessarily opposed to procedural and structural reforms within the House, but they consider them to be inadequate and unnecessarily insular in the context of wider political problems. Instead, they now argue for major transformative reforms, external to the House.

'External' reformers emerged as a significant force in the mid-1970s. Worsening economic conditions (rising unemployment, stagnant production, burgeoning inflation) were aggravated by political instability: the uncertain outcome of the two general elections of 1974 and the relative desertion by voters of the two main parties. Some analysts viewed the nation's problems as having a political as well as an economic base. Part of the problem was deemed to be the adversary, two-party system.[19] Two parties competed vigorously for the all-or-nothing spoils of a general election victory. Once in office, a party proceeded to carry out an ambitious programme, a programme put together to out-promise the opponent party and one likely to run up against the constraints of limited resources once an attempt was made to implement it. At a later election, the opponent party was likely to be returned and then proceed to reverse the policies of its predecessor. The consequences of this were policy discontinuity, government overload and increasing disenchantment with a government unable to deliver on its promises. The outcome of the two 1974 elections demonstrated that the electoral system could not necessarily produce a clear majority for a government – considered to be one of the main attractions by proponents of the existing system – and electoral trends sugggested the declining relevance of the Conservative and Labour Parties. The 1974 elections – and that of 1983 – revealed effective multi-party competition. The two-party system was thus part of the problem; and that system was no longer proving capable of delivering the advantages previously ascribed to it.

On this analysis, both government effectiveness and consent for the political system are undermined. Reforming the procedures of the House of Commons to enhance its scrutinizing capacity would not constitute a solution to problems seen as inherent in the political system. Rather, a solution is seen in the introduction of a new electoral system. One based on proportional representation would, it is argued, have beneficial consequences for both effectiveness and consent. A system of PR, ensuring proportionality between the percentage of votes cast and the percentage of seats won, would constitute a fairer electoral system and, by being seen as such, would enhance consent for the political system. By denying any one party an overall majority in the House of Commons (no one party having achieved an absolute majority of the votes cast since 1935) the iniquities of the present one-party hegemony in government would be avoided. On the basis of current electoral trends, no one party would achieve an overall majority; a government would probably have to be formed by a coalition incorporating one or more centrist parties. If a fairly stable coalition were to be formed, it would probably achieve sufficient electoral support to ensure continuity in office and thus continuity in policy. Hence government effectiveness would be enhanced. Furthermore, this would not be at the expense of the House of Commons. Proportional representation would allow electors greater freedom of choice between candidates. 'Voters . . . can elect a more independent or "rebel" member of a party if they wish. So no party machine can "discipline" any Member by depriving him of his seat.'[20] Greater independence on the part of Members would be more congenial to the operation of investigative select committees and would serve to reinvigorate the House as an effective body of scrutiny and influence.

Other – sometimes the same – reformers see a partial solution in the devolution of certain powers and responsibilities to elected assemblies in Scotland, Wales and the English regions.[21] Devolution would serve to alleviate the pressure on and the demands made of central government, thus serving as a solution to the problem of overload. By allowing decisions to be made on a more informed regional basis, by bodies elected on a local basis, government would be not only more efficient but also enjoy greater support. A number of other reformers advocate the introduction of an entrenched Bill of Rights. Led in the 1970s by Lord Hailsham, they emphasised the power accruing to the executive through control of a compliant parliamentary majority.[22] Instead of directing their prescriptions to changing the structure or composition of Parliament, they sought instead to put certain basic rights beyond the reach of a simple (partisan and shifting) parliamentary majority. The most favoured means of achieving their goal was the incorporation into British law of the European Convention on Human Rights, with any subsequent legislation that conflicted with its provisions to be struck down by the courts.

These reforms are not mutually exclusive. Indeed, a number of 'external' reformers, notably the Liberals, have embraced all three.[23] They became prominent in political debate in the latter half of the 1970s. The Labour government of James Callaghan sought, unsuccessfully, to introduce devolution for Scotland and Wales. The House of Lords actually passed a Bill of Rights in successive sessions. The return of a Conservative government in 1979 took much of the wind out of the reformers' sails. The government adopted a position that was either hostile or generally non-committal on all three proposed reforms.[24] Nonetheless, pressure for reform continues. Electoral reform constitutes a major plank of the SDP/Liberal Alliance and is expected to constitute the essential condition of the Alliance joining a coalition government should it hold the balance of power in a future hung Parliament. With the exception of the Conservative Party, all main political parties are committed now to a policy of devolution.

Like the internal reformers, the external reformers are not free of critics. Indeed, a number of weighty criticisms have been levelled against them. Advocates of electoral reform have seen their analysis and prescription countered on both practical and intellectual grounds. According to some critics, including this writer, electoral reform could threaten effectiveness *and* consent.

A change in the electoral system is not likely in the foreseeable future. At the 1983 general election, the Alliance parties obtained nearly 26 per cent of the votes cast for less than 4 per cent of the seats in the House of Commons. It was a result that added weight to the case for reform and gave added impetus to the Alliance parties in arguing for it. Yet that very same result also worked against its acceptance. The Conservative and Labour parties benefited clearly from the existing system and so are unwilling to jettison it; the results robbed the Alliance of a significant parliamentary platform from which to push the case for reform. Stuart Walkland in 1983 quoted Ron Hayward as having written that 'with PR would vanish all our hopes of a socialist Britain'. According to Walkland, 'no better statement of the willingness of the major parties to distort democracy for ideological ends can be found'.[25] Such a contentious – and contestable – assertion (perish the thought that other parties might indulge in such distortion) nonetheless points to the unlikelihood of the major parties concurring in the introduction of a system of proportional representation.

More significantly, the reformers' argument appears flawed. The assumptions upon which they proceed – notably that voting patterns would be similar under a PR system to those that exist under the first-past-the-post system – are not necessarily well founded; they are, of necessity, empirically untested. Nor is it clear that PR would have the consequences that they posit. It is sheer speculation as to the form of government that might result. If one accepts that no one party will achieve an absolute majority of seats, then there are three possibilities. One is minority government, one party seeking to govern without the support of another party. Experiences of minority government in Britain do nothing to suggest that such a system would increase effectiveness or consent; rather, the reverse. Another possibility is weak coalition government, partners to the coalition shifting over time. Again, effectiveness and consent are not likely to be enhanced: government would have problems in maintaining continuity in policy and, given post-election shifts in the composition of the coalition, would not be able to claim greater support from the electoral majority. The third and final possibility would be strong coalition government, a coalition sufficient to ensure electoral support that would maintain it in office for a considerable period of time. Such a form of government could increase effectiveness, avoiding policy discontinuity, but might by its very nature jeopardize the maintenance of consent.

In what ways would the latter two possibilities (weak, shifting coalition or strong, continuing coalitions) jeopardize consent for the political system? A shifting coalition, involving post-election bargaining, could (indeed *would* if parties have not made their intentions clear at the preceding election) produce a government which enjoyed the definitive support of not one elector. Suppose, for example, that the Conservatives contest an election as a single party, with a manifesto they as a party intend to implement if returned to office, and the Liberals do likewise. What if the Conservatives obtain 40 per cent of the popular vote and the Liberals obtain 25 per cent, neither achieving therefore a majority of seats, and then agree between themselves to enter into a coalition? Does not this Conservative-Liberal coalition enjoy the support of 65 per cent of the electors? No. It enjoys the clearly expressed support of not one elector. There is no authoritative evidence that at the election any elector cast a vote for a Con–Lib coalition. (That is, 40 per cent voted Conservative, 25 per cent voted Liberal, no one voted Con-Lib.) Unless parties make clear their intentions during or prior to the election, they can make no claim to electoral support in the event of entering into a coalition. A coalition enjoying the definitive support of no electors can hardly maintain a claim to enhance support for the political system.

A near-permanent coalition could threaten consent by excluding continuously one party from office. That party could enjoy the support of a greater number of electors than the number who feel excluded (and, in the case of some, alienated) under the existing plurality method of voting. Under the existing system, one of the two parties enjoying in combination the support of 70 per cent or more of voters stand a chance of being returned to office; under PR, a party continuously in office with, say, 55 per cent of the popular vote would result in a greater number of 'excluded' voters. If certain significant forces are excluded in effect from government then, as Michael Keating has noted, the prospects of extra-parliamentary action would be increased significantly.[26] Hence, far from increasing consent, PR could result in an undermining of consent; and, if severe, could then threaten the capacity of government to govern. Thus, in the long run, effectiveness as well as consent would be under threat.

Furthermore, the reformers' contentions as to the effect of PR for the Commons do not go unchallenged. A government able to ensure policy continuity (through a parliamentary majority) and greater independence of Members of Parliament are not logically compatible. It is not certain that PR would encourage greater independence of parties. Much would depend upon the electoral system chosen to replace the present one. Under a coalition government, bargaining may remain confined to Members of the governing coalition, excluding members of the opposition parties and so further threatening the maintenance of consent. Cohesion could remain a feature of parliamentary life, coalition Members being called upon to maintain the coalition (and themselves) in office. Indeed, as Hugh Berrington has pointed out, the introduction of PR might actually serve to increase discipline at Westminster 'by enabling moderate MPs to defy their local parties, and to express their loyalty to the parliamentary leadership in the division lobbies'.[27] Hence, it is possible that none of the reformers' goals in terms of effectiveness, consent or better parliamentary scrutiny would be achieved. Their failure could do far greater, and probably irreparable, damage to the British polity than that inflicted by the present electoral system. Thus one should not take the risk.

Devolution and an entrenched Bill of Rights attract vigorous criticism as well. The case for a Bill of Rights is vulnerable on various grounds.[28] There is no agreement on the rights to be entrenched. Indeed, some consensus on basic rights is a prerequisite for the introduction of a Bill of Rights; yet it is the very lack of consensus (indeed, increasing disagreement) which has led to calls for an entrenched Bill of Rights. The reformers thus find themselves in a Catch-22 position. (With a consensus, why the need to entrench those rights on which there is agreement? Without a consensus, one lacks the basis to introduce a Bill of Rights). There is no agreement on the method by which an entrenched measure could be introduced. It thus appears that the introduction of a Bill of Rights is not possible. Critics would suggest that it would not be desirable either. It would put certain rights beyond the purview of a simple parliamentary majority, trusting them instead to the tender care of the courts. In so doing, it would thrust the judiciary further into the political fray, probably undermining respect not only for the courts but for the political system as a whole. If Parliament is not strong enough to defend basic rights, then critics of a Bill of Rights contend that the answer is to strengthen the elected Parliament and not the unelected courts.[29]

Similarly, devolution might threaten consent and also effectiveness. It could lead to a greater economic disparity between regions. Richer regions would probably become richer and poorer regions much poorer. Under the existing centralized system, Whitehall is conscious of the territorial dimension of British politics and works to ensure some measure of equity. A point made during the devolution debates of the 1970s was that Scotland and Wales have received more favourable treatment than their small populations would normally justify. An exacerbation of regional disparity would increase disaffection with government. And electing the regional assemblies would do little to overcome this. Why elect a regional assembly if it lacks the resources sufficient to maintain its policy commitments? Indeed, regionalism could add to the problems by adding an extra burdensome layer of government to that which currently exists.[30] Nor would some degree of regional autonomy serve to protect civil liberties – one of the claims made by some of its supporters. In the United States, as Duane Lockard has argued, federalism has served as an agent for the maintenance of racial discrimination.[31] Regional governments, one may presume, would have a natural tendency to reflect regional prejudices.

Radical, transformative reform, in short, might do more damage than that which it seeks to repair. Indeed, there is a danger that the proposed cure could actually kill the patient. Walkland has characterized the prescriptions of some of the internal reformers as being akin to using sticking plasters to treat a broken leg. His diagnosis could well be assailed for unnecessarily magnifying the scale of the problem. Indeed, his diagnosis appears to have been undertaken at a somewhat detached level. Much of his basic argument lacks empirical foundation. Citing Samuel Beer and a disaffected former Labour MP, he asserts: 'the truth is that individuals and groups have lost fundamental trust in the political process'.[32] This 'truth' is so self-evident that no figures are presented to support it. This may be because there is little empirical evidence to suggest overwhelming lack of trust in the political process and none to suggest a significant decline in trust over the past decade or so.[33] I do not contest the assertion that *some* groups and individuals have lost trust in the political process. But are they any greater than the number whose trust could be threatened by the consequences that could result from the introduction of proportional representation for parliamentary elections?

And what of foreign experience? Walkland asserts that 'some two-party systems have shown an enviable capacity for development and self-renewal – that of the USA is a prime example'. Some systems may have such a capacity. The USA is certainly not one of them. Indeed, some American observers in the 1970s still looked to the British party model as one to be emulated.[34] The inaccuracy of Walkland's statement is, however, not what is important. The point to be stressed is that foreign experience provides little useful guide to what could or should be done in Britain. Misreading of the position abroad serves merely to exacerbate the problem. One could cite certain political systems as examples of stable PR systems; others could be said to demonstrate political instability. It is a largely futile exercise. Foreign experience may serve to sensitize us to certain difficulties and nuances, but it should not be taken further than that, at least not in this instance. Lack of similarities precludes generalization.

Political structures exist within specific political cultures; they have usually influenced, and themselves been largely shaped by, those cultures. To wrench those structures from the political cultures in which they reside, and where they are integrated with other structures, and seek to transpose them to an alien political culture is a potentially disastrous exercise: witness the experience of the Westminster model of government in the former British colonies of Africa. Reform of the British political system has to be seen within the context of the British political culture. And that culture, I would suggest, needs a more careful and long-term evaluation than it has been accorded to date by the external reformers.[35]

The House of Lords

Reference to the British political culture brings us most appropriately to the House of Lords. No other industrialized or developed nation has an upper chamber based on the hereditary principle. It is a striking feature of British political history that a House based on traditional authority has survived, largely intact, the transition to a form of government based on rational–legal authority.

Since the growth of a mass electorate in the nineteenth century, the House has appeared anomalous, an apparently indefensible and anachronistic element of the institutional structure of British government. It has, in consequence, been the focus of numerous schemes of reform. Almost a century before Bernard Crick wrote *The Reform of Parliament*, John Stuart Mill and Walter Bagehot were propounding suggestions for reforming the Upper House, with Bagehot worrying that it might never be reformed. Reform ideas have come from all parts of the political spectrum. As Crick pointed out, the fifth Marquess of Salisbury proposed even more schemes of reform than the Fabian Society. Some significant reforms have been implemented, most notably the limitation of the legislative delaying power (the 1911 and 1949 Parliament Acts) and the introduction of life peers (the 1958 Life Peerages Act). But its hereditary basis, its consequent limited powers and its limitations in exercising a scrutinizing function have made the Upper House a continuing target of parliamentary reformers. Reform proposals continue to emanate from all parts of the political spectrum and to take disparate forms.

Approaches to reform of the Lords can be grouped under four headings, the four Rs: retain, reform, replace, and remove altogether.[36] Those who wish to retain the House as it is defend the hereditary principle as the backbone of the independence of the House: they are prepared to discuss reform in terms only of procedural change. Those who favour reform of the existing House advocate in particular the phasing out of the voting power of hereditary peers – the approach on which the ill-fated 1969 Parliament (No. 2) Bill was based. Those who favour reform of the procedures and composition of the existing House can be characterized as internal reformers; they seek to work within or to adapt the existing structure. Those who seek to replace or remove altogether the Upper House comprise the 'external' reformers. Those who wish to replace the House as it currently exists favour in particular a directly or indirectly elected second chamber. Those who wish to remove it altogether are unicameralists.

Reform from within

Proposals for procedural and internal structural changes have come, in particular, from within the House. They have emanated from committees of the House as well as from individual peers.

The House has variously considered reports from its Procedure Committee. In the 1979–83 Parliament, for example, it considered three such reports.[37] The recommendations emanating from the committee have not been radical. They have covered such matters as the definition of a backbencher for the purposes of short debates and the length of Question Time on starred questions. Their recommendations have been accepted by the House, usually without extensive debate.

Far more significant in content, if not effect, was the First Report from the Select Committee on Practice and Procedure, published in April 1977. The committee had before it a memorandum from the European Communities Committee recommending the establishment of a series of select committees to scrutinize the activities of government departments. A similar proposal had been made by the Clerk of the House. He envisaged seven or eight sessional committees, each comprising about 12 peers, covering particular policy areas. Each committee, he thought, could scrutinize proposals in Bills, delegated legislation, and White and Green Papers. The initial scrutiny of each Bill would be of the same kind as that undertaken by the sub-committees of the European Communities Committee. 'This scheme envisages an approach to domestic legislation similar to that of the European Communities Committee to Community legislation. . . . the Committee have concluded that the adoption of the suggested committee structure would be of considerable benefit, and they recommend the proposal to the House.'[38] Like the report of the parallel committee in the Commons – both committees were appointed in 1976, but the Commons' committee reported in 1978[39] – the proposal for such committees constituted the most significant and radical of its various recommendations.

Proposals for reform have emanated from peers on all sides of the House. Lord Alport has advocated different sessional periods for each House (to give the Lords longer at the end of a session to consider legislation); Lord Denham, now the government chief whip, has advocated a minimum standard for gaps between the stages of Bills; and Lord Aylestone has proposed the earlier tabling of amendments.[40] Five peers recommended to the Procedure and Practice Committee the creation of a Foreign Affairs Select Committee, a recommendation that found favour with the committee in its Second Report in 1977 (though it suggested that the House should wait to see what the Commons proposed to do);[41] more radically – and less realistically – Lord Aylestone has voiced the hope that the House could have a sabbatical year in which there was no legislation at all ('but I cannot see any Government agreeing to that') and, in the same debate, Lord Paget suggested in all seriousness that, in order to encourage consensus, peers refrain from voting.[42] Other recommendations emanating from individual peers have ranged from joint meetings of both Houses on certain important issues to improved conditions of service for front-bench spokesmen. The reforms suggested, then, are disparate. None of those mentioned has been implemented.

There are two types of criticism that can be levelled at the proposals for internal reform. They parallel the criticisms levelled at internal reforms in the Commons. One concerns the means for achieving it; the other concerns its relevance.

If procedural and structural changes are to be made, the political will has to exist among peers to achieve them. As we have seen (chapters 5 and 6), the House has witnessed an attitudinal change on the part of peers over the past decade. That change, however, has to be taken further if serious reforms are to be pursued. During the Lords' debate on the First Report from the Procedure and Practice Committee, the Leader of the House, Lord Peart, conceded that there was 'a strong current of opinion in favour of an experiment to try out the Select Committee's recommendation for scrutiny procedure'.[43] Rather than accept a motion to implement the committee's recommendation for a series of committees, he proposed that the House concede the case for an experiment and that the matter be referred to the regular Procedure Committee 'for detailed consideration of the problems involved'.[44] On that basis, the peer who had tabled the motion – Lord Windlesham – withdrew it. In the event, Lord Peart appeared to lose interest in pursuing the matter (in the opinion of one observer, he 'ratted') and the Procedure Committee found itself in some disarray on the subject. Rather than pursue the recommendations of the Practice and Procedure Committee, it opted instead for a proposal from two peers for the creation of a Science and Technology Committee. Hence the Select Committee on Science and Technology, but no series of domestic scrutiny committees. Peers have not pressed the issue since. A Practice and Procedure Committee was not appointed in the 1979 Parliament. No major reform proposals have come from the Procedure Committee. If the House is to undertake major structural and procedural reforms, peers have to be prepared to press for them – in the same way that MPs pressed for the new select committees. Some members of the government front bench are not unsympathetic to reform and might well be willing to respond to pressure from other noble lords. If such committees are to be established, peers have to press for them and, once established, sustain them in the same way in which they have sustained the European Communities Committee.

The other criticism comes from those not particularly sympathetic to procedural reform. To them, such reforms are irrelevant. Procedural improvements cannot alter the fact that the House lacks any claim to be a representative institution. (Peers represent no one but themselves: their writs of summons are personal to them.) The House lacks the political clout, and hence the sanctions, that would flow from being able to claim such a status. To many critics, the House constitutes an unacceptable second chamber, lacking the legitimacy necessary for it to fulfil a major scrutinizing function. What is needed, according to these critics, is a reform based on composition rather than procedures.

What might be termed one branch of the internal-reform school favours a change based on the existing membership, the hereditary peers being deprived of the power to vote (though, for existing peers, not the right to attend and speak), voting power residing only in life peers and hereditary peers of first creation. This, it is believed, would buttress the legitimacy of the House without radical change and without jeopardizing those tasks which the House currently fulfils. This was the approach adopted in 1969 when the Parliament (No. 2) Bill was introduced. The Bill fell foul of sustained backbench opposition in the Commons. Had it reached the Lords, it is thought certain that it would have passed.

Radical reformers wish to go further. To them, even a modified House of *Lords* is unacceptable. They want either a new chamber or no chamber at all.

External reformers

To external reformers, a hereditary or an appointed House lacks popular legitimacy. Without that, it cannot fulfil adequately the functions ascribed to a second chamber. Many of those who concede the need for a second chamber to undertake scrutiny of measures coming from the Commons argue for an elected chamber (Senate being a popular name for the new body). Such a chamber would be elected either on a national, multi-member PR basis or elected on a regional basis, the latter proposal finding favour with many devolutionists. Once elected, it would provide a chamber with a legitimacy to parallel that of the Commons and thus have the basis to undertake an effective scrutinizing function.[45]

For others, the unicameralists, a second chamber is not necessary. The functions ascribed to Parliament – the provision of ministers, legitimization, scrutiny and influence – can just as well be undertaken by one (reformed and effficient) chamber. Hence one abolishes the House of Lords and then proceeds not to replace it, but instead to reform the House of Commons. To such abolitionists, a second chamber constitutes more of a hindrance than a help in fulfilling the tasks of a Parliament. As Lord Wedderburn succinctly put it: 'Either the second chamber is less democratic than the Commons in which case it should not be able to delay legislation, or it is just as democratic, when there is no point in having two chambers'.[46] To Tony Benn and others, the House of Lords is an anachronism in need of an early demise.

Proposals for an elected second chamber are not new. The preamble to the 1911 Parliament Act envisaged a popularly elected chamber. Abolition has variously been canvassed. It has gained prominence in recent years, the Labour Party Conference having adopted abolition as party policy. Yet a number of problems exist with such reform proposals. An elected second chamber would enhance consent, but at the risk of effectiveness. It would enjoy the same political authority as that of the Commons (possibly more on the argument for PR) and two coequal chambers could engender stalemate in the event of a conflict between the two. Potentially it could pose a major problem for government seeking to achieve approval of its measures. The abolition of the Upper House would place a major burden on the House of Commons. There is no evidence that the Lower House would necessarily be able to cope with that burden. What research has been done suggests that to leave it all to the Commons 'would prove detrimental to the legislative process as a whole'.[47] Abolition could contribute to Hailsham's feared 'elective dictatorship' by removing a constitutional longstop; but, if the legislative process were to topple under the strain, it could endanger government effectiveness and, in the long run, consent for the political system. Indeed, effectiveness and consent could also be threatened in that abolition could lead to the demise of parliamentary sovereignty.[48] Parliamentary sovereignty is a judicially self-imposed doctrine. It rests on the existence of 'Parliament'. With one chamber of Parliament removed, it is not certain that the courts would recognize the Commons alone (or, technically, the Commons and the Crown) as constituting 'Parliament'. Hence, they might cease to accept the supremacy of statute law. The effect would be to strengthen the position of the courts and add a powerful new judicial dimension to the political process. Such a development could, in the British political culture, undermine both effectiveness (government measures subject to invalidation by the courts) and consent (the consequence of political decisions being taken by unelected judges). The effect, in short, could be completely the reverse of that intended by the proponents of reform.

In both Houses, then, the reforms canvassed have their merits. They also have demerits. Each has sufficient grounds to justify its place in the reform debate. Being discussed, though, is a necessary but not sufficient condition for implementation. Of the reforms proposed, are we likely to see any carried out in the near future? Or are the opponents of reform likely to win by default?

Where To From Here?

In practical terms, radical transformative reforms are unlikely to be achieved. A number of reformers are moving in the direction of discussing the constitution in broad terms and putting together a package of reforms. Such packages[49] enjoy some degree of coherence but, as packages, little chance of success. Even if implemented, singly or in combination, radical reforms are not likely to realize the reformers' dreams. A comparative approach has its dangers – at least when used selectively, as in discussing electoral systems – but it also has its uses (see chapter 1). It may provide some guide, and allow of generalization, as to the trends and as to what is possible. In common with most other West European and major Commonwealth countries, Britain has a 'reactive' (or policy-influencing) legislature.[50] To transform it to an 'active' (or policy-making) legislature on the American model (the US providing the only example of such a national legislature) would require more radical changes than most reformers, except for *The Economist*,[51] are prepared to contemplate. Such reforms would include, for example, a formal separation of powers between the executive and the legislative branches. This, to put it mildly, is not a feasible reform. It is also undesirable. Emulating American experience would jeopardize government effectiveness (allowing for conflict between the two branches) at a time when to do so could be disastrous. It would also be alien to the political culture.

All one could, and should, realistically hope for is to make Parliament a more effective policy-influencer. The changes of recent years have made a modest but by no means insignificant contribution to that. More needs to be done. Radical reforms are unlikely to come about and, as I have argued, are not necessarily sustainable on the merits of the argument. In terms of their implications for effectiveness and consent, they are potentially dangerous. Changes have to be wrought – in both Houses – by parliamentarians themselves. As we have seen, there has been a change of attitude in both Houses over the past decade. MPs and peers have adopted a more participatory attitude: they want to be more involved in the political process. A large government majority in the Commons may actually encourage such a participatory attitude. Eager government backbenchers, the number exceeding the government jobs likely to be available, may seek outlets for their frustrated energies and ambitions. Active peers, realizing that their House faces no prospect of early reform, appear keen to get on with the task of scrutiny. What is needed, very badly, is for these prevailing attitudes to be exploited and for MPs and peers to go further down the road of procedural and structural reform.

The most cogent and succinct statement in favour of such reform, putting it within a political context, was that made by Lord Fulton in a Lords' debate in 1977. His Lordship's comments apply just as well to the Commons as to the Lords:

Of course we are a political House with only two Lobbies, not a research institute, a super Brookings; not are we required alone to shoulder the responsibility for building the new Jerusalem. But is there not a strong case for us to recognise the need in the management of our own business to do what we are specially well qualified to do, to give some of our minds to the more distant horizons of our times and to provide ourselves with appropriate instruments to help in laying the foundations on which those who have to take decisions can more safely build?[52]

In seeking to realize such a goal, there is no reason why reforms should be confined to marginal improvements of existing procedures. The Commons might well consider the more extensive use of special standing committees and a major reform of its legislative procedure. In a memorandum to the Select Committee on Procedure in late 1984, the legislative study group of the Study of Parliament Group advocated a package encompassing automatic timetabling, the greater use of special standing committees (the recommendation concerning whether or not to employ them resting, by convention, with opposition parties) and a provision for the carry-over of Bills from one session to another.[53] Other reforms are worthy of consideration. The Procedure Committee itself made an encouraging start in deciding to proceed on the basis of its wider remit, rather than confining itself to consideration of the length of speeches and committee-stage scrutiny. The committee could give a significant lead to the House. (Whether it does so remains – at the time of writing – to be seen.) By building on recent changes, the House could move towards being a better scrutinizing body. Procedural change remains necessary. So too does an improvement in pay and facilities (see appendix 2). The two need to be achieved simultaneously.

Likewise with the House of Lords. The House is making greater, and more effective, use of committees than hitherto. It may move further in the direction of using sessional committees to scrutinize sectors of domestic (as opposed to European Communities) policy. It has the expertise in terms of members. Indeed, as was shown in chapter 6, the authority of Lords' committees derives largely from the expertise of their members. But those members, to do the job properly, will require the facilities (and the recompense) appropriate to the task.

To external reformers, such changes may seem marginal, indeed irrelevant. But they are practical, achievable reforms. In combination, they could make a significant contribution to Parliament's capacity to serve as a body of scrutiny and influence, doing so without jeopardizing the balance between effectiveness and consent necessary for the continued well-being of the British polity.

Notes

1 E. Powell, 'Parliament and the Question of Reform', *Teaching Politics*, 11(2), May 1982, p. 172.
2 G. Almond and S. Verba, *The Civic Culture* (Princeton: Princeton University Press, 1963), p. 102.
3 Granada Television, *The State of the Nation* (London: Granada Television, 1973), p. 201.
4 P. Kellner, 'Who Runs Britain?' *Sunday Times*, 18 September 1977.
5 See P. Norton, *The British Polity* (London: Longman, 1984), pp. 359–63.
6 An ORC poll in 1977 found that respondents gave constitutional change 'a very low priority' in relation to other issues: S. E. Finer, *The Changing British Party System 1945–79* (Washington DC: American Enterprise Institute, 1980), p. 176.
7 See especially ch. 12 in S. A. Walkland and M. Ryle (eds), *The Commons Today* (London: Fontana, 1981), and S. A. Walkland, 'Parliamentary

Reform, Party Realignment and Electoral Reform', in D. Judge (ed.), *The Politics of Parliamentary Reform* (London: Heinemann, 1983), 37–53.

8 Developed in P. Norton, 'Committees in the British House of Commons', paper prepared for Committee of Co-operation for European Parliamentary Studies, 1984.

9 See P. Norton, *The Commons in Perspective* (Oxford: Martin Robertson, 1981), pp. 205–7.

10 See the comments in P. Norton, 'The Norton View', in Judge, *The Politics of Parliamentary Reform*, p. 58.

11 *First Report from the Select Committee on Procedure, Session 1977/78*, HC 588–1 (London: HMSO, 1978).

12 All-Party House of Commons' Reform Group, *Findings of the Survey of MPs' Attitudes to Reform and the Role of the MP* (London: mimeo, 1984).

13 See *First Report from the Select Committee on Procedure, Session 1977/78*, HC 588–1 and HC 588–2 (London: HMSO, 1978), and *First Report from the Select Committee on Procedure (Supply), Session 1980/81*, HC 118 (London: HMSO, 1981).

14 *First Report from the Select Committee on Procedure*, vol II: Minutes of Evidence, p. 18.

15 As, for example, E. du Cann, *Parliament and the Purse Strings* (London: Conservative Political Centre, 1977), and B. George and B. Evans, 'Parliamentary Reform: The Internal View', in Judge, *The Politics of Parliamentary Reform*, pp. 70–95.

16 Similar calls – for increased staff – have been made by other Members and by the chairmen of some of the select committees. See, for example, *The First Report from the Liaison Committee, Session 1982/83*, HC 92 (London: HMSO, 1982), pp. 49, 65 and 80.

17 *HC Deb.* 28, col. 141.

18 This point derives from and is developed in Norton, 'The Norton View', in Judge, *The Politics of Parliamentary Reform*, pp. 54–69.

19 See especially S. E. Finer (ed.), *Adversary Politics and Electoral Reform* (London: Wigram, 1975); D. Coombes, *Representative Government and Economic Power* (London: Heinemann, 1982); SDP/Liberal Alliance, *Electoral Reform* (London: SDP/Liberal Alliance, 1982); and S. A. Walkland, 'Parliamentary Reform, Party Realignment and Electoral Reform', in Judge, *The Politics of Parliamentary Reform*, pp. 37–53. See also V. Bogdanor, *What is Proportional Representation?* (Oxford: Martin Robertson, 1983).

20 'Fair Voting is Safer' *ER Leaflet No. 40* (London: Electoral Reform Society, n.d).

21 See especially *The Royal Commission on the Constitution*, vol. I: Report, Cmnd 5640 (London: HMSO, 1973), D. Owen, *Face the Future* (Oxford: Oxford University Press, 1981), and V. Bogdanor, *Devolution* (Oxford: Oxford University Press, 1979).

22 See Lord Hailsham, *Elective Dictatorship* (London: BBC, 1976) and, by the same author, *The Dilemma of Democracy* (London: Collins, 1978).

23 See, for example, the Liberal Party's Reform of Government Panel, *A New Constitutional Settlement* (London: Liberal Publications Department, 1980), and the summary which appears in A. W. Bradley, 'Proposals for Constitutional Reform', *Public Law*, Winter 1982, pp. 529–34.

24 See the comments of Timothy Raison in the House of Commons, *HC Deb.* 2, cols 1262–4.

25 Walkland, 'Parliamentary Reform', p. 51.

26 Quoted in the conclusion to Judge, *The Politics of Parliamentary Reform*, p. 184.

27 H. Berrington, 'Electoral Reform and National Government', in Finer, *Adversary Politics and Electoral Reform*, p. 279. This quote also appears in Judge, *The Politics of Parliamentary Reform*, at p. 183.

28 These points are developed in P. Norton, *The Constitution in Flux* (Oxford: Martin Robertson, 1982), ch. 13.

29 See, for example, R. Kilroy-Silk MP, 'Wrongs of a Bill of Rights', *The Guardian*, 4 February 1977.

30 Norton, *The Constitution in Flux*, p. 184.

31 D. Lockard, *The Perverted Priorities of American Politics*, 2nd edn (London: Collier Macmillan, 1976), pp. 90–106.

32 Walkland, 'Parliamentary Reform', p. 48.

33 See Norton, *The British Polity*, pp. 360–1.

34 See, for example, C. M. Hardin, *Presidential Power and Accountability: Towards a New Constitution* (Chicago: University of Chicago Press, 1974), p. 139.

35 This point is argued at greater length in Norton, *The British Polity*, ch. 15.

36 This categorization is made and developed in Norton, *The Constitution in Flux*, ch. 6.

37 See *HL Deb.* 426, cols 705–9; *HL Deb.* 427, cols 1289–90; and *HL Deb.* 440, cols 1234–5.

38 *First Report from the Select Committee of the House of Lords on Practice and Procedure*, HL 141 (London: HMSO, 1977), paras 47 and 52.

39 The two committees had power to meet concurrently, but did not exercise it. They did, however, exchange papers.

40 *First Report from the Select Committee on Practice and Procedure*, pp. 68, 76, and *HL Deb.* 385, col. 205.

41 *Second Report from the Select Committee on Practice and Procedure*, HL 256 (London: HMSO, 1977), pp. ix–x, 1–7.

42 *HL Deb.* 385, col. 243.

43 *HL Deb.* 385, col. 261.

44 Ibid.

45 For a development of the argument, see Norton, *The Constitution in Flux*, pp. 123–5. Some reformers also favour an Upper House based on functional representation.

46 Quoted in H. Hebert, 'The Lords Under the Microscope'. *The Guardian*, 1 March 1979.

47 N. Baldwin, 'The Abolition of the House of Lords: The Effect on the

House of Commons and the Legislative Process', paper presented at the annual conference of the Political Studies Association, University of Hull, April 1981, p. 27.

48 Norton, *The Constitution in Flux*. p. 129.

49 See, for example, N. Johnson, *In Search of the Constitution* (London: Methuen, 1980), and the Liberal Party's Reform of Government Panel, *A New Constitutional Settlement* (London: Liberal Publications Department, 1980). See also Bradley, 'Proposals for Constitutional Reform'.

50 For the definition of a 'reactive' legislature, see M. Mezey, *Comparative Legislatures* (Durham NC: Duke University Press, 1979); for a discussion of 'Policy-influencing' legislatures, see P. Norton, 'Parliament and Policy in Britain: The House of Commons as a Policy Influencer', *Teaching Politics* 13(2), May 1984.

51 In an editorial, 'Blowing up a Tyranny', on 5 November 1977, *The Economist* advocated not only a formal separation of powers but also federalism, electoral reform, the setting up of a constitutional court, and a number of other constitutional departures. It omitted to mention how these changes were to be brought about.

52 *HL Deb.* 385, col. 211.

53 *Select Committee on Procedure: Session 1984/85.* Public Bill Procedure: Minutes of Evidence, 18 December 1984, HC 49–iv (London: Her Majesty's Stationery Office, 1984).

Appendix 1

Recent Structural and Procedural Changes in the House of Commons

Philip Norton

Speaking in the House of Lords in 1977, Lord O'Hagan declared: 'Parliament dies if it does not update its procedures. Procedures are the muscle and sinew of Parliament. If we do not exercise that muscle and keep it in good trim for contemporary challenges then we shall have no real job left to do'.[1] In recent years, both Houses of Parliament have witnessed significant changes in their structures and procedures. The most important in the House of Lords have been considered already (chapter 6). The best known of those in the House of Commons have also been covered (chapter 3). However, the Commons has witnessed a variety of procedural reforms. Some have been essentially minor and of no great interest to the student of politics.[2] Others have been noteworthy, modifying or adding to procedures known to the student. They can be summarized under the following headings.

Select committees

By far the best-known structural reform has been the introduction of the departmentally related select committees, appointed by the House in 1979 'to examine the expenditure, administration and policy in the principal government departments . . . and associated public bodies'. In January 1980 a Liaison Select Committee, comprising the chairmen of the committees (and some additional members), was appointed.

The select committees were reappointed in the new Parliament returned in 1983. The committees have been considered already in detail (chapter 3). In the Commons' Reform Group survey of MPs in 1984, almost 60 per cent of respondents rated the select committees as being successful (or very successful). Only 3.2 per cent of respondents considered them a 'comparative failure'.[3]

Special standing committees

Beginning in the 1980/1 session, the House has witnessed an experiment with the appointment of a number of special standing committees. Such committees were recommended by the Select Committee on Procedure in its 1978 report.

Under the procedure involved, a Bill may be sent to a committee which constitutes, in effect, a hybrid of a select and a standing committee. The special standing committee (SSC) can sit as a select committee and examine witnesses (it can hold three 1½-hour public sessions) before reverting to the traditional standing committee format to examine the Bill clause by clause.

In commending the new procedure, the Leader of the House envisaged that it would be employed particularly in the case of 'Government Bills, which raise substantial issues . . . not of acute party controversy'. In the remainder of that Parliament, four Bills were sent to SSCs: the Criminal Attempts Bill, the Education Bill, the Deep Sea Mining (Temporary Provisions) Bill (all in the 1980/1 session) and the Mental Health Amendment Bill (in the 1981/2 session). In the first session of the present Parliament, one Bill – on matrimonial proceedings – was referred to an SSC.

The experience of the committees has proved popular with Members appointed to serve on them. A survey of MPs who served on the first three SSCs found that, of 37 respondents, 28 felt that the SSC experiment had been 'very worthwhile' and only one said that it made no difference.[4] The SSC on the Criminal Attempts Bill was considered by Members involved to have demonstrated the special value of the procedure. Representatives of various affected groups – the Law Society, the police, the judiciary, the National Council for Civil Liberties – appeared before the committee and as a result of the representations made, four substantive amendments to the Bill were made. The whole of the first clause had to be redrafted following criticism from an academic witness to the effect that it was unworkable as it stood.

The value of special standing committees has been queried on the grounds that the procedure merely allows for 'insider' groups to make representations that they would normally make to government and that the criticisms of the Criminal Attempts Bill would probably have been taken into account earlier by government had the Bill not been rushed and some confusion existed as to the new procedure.[5] However, there is much to be said for a procedure which brings out into the open the representations that are normally made in private to government by 'insider' groups. The SSCs also have the potential to allow 'outsider' groups to make their views known in an authoritative forum. They may also provide a structured and open forum in which amendments to Bills may be suggested by affected groups, an advantage over the current untidy and questionable practice of groups seeking to proffer amendments via sympathetic MPs, MPs who do not always reveal the genesis of the amendments.

Estimates Days

In 1981, the Select Committee on Procedure (Supply) recomended that there should be eight days a session when the Estimates could be debated and voted upon (something which was not then possible). In July 1982 the House approved three full days to be set aside each session to discuss the Estimates, and for the Estimates for discussion to be chosen not by the government's business managers but by the Liaison Select Committee.

The first Estimates Day was held in the following session. On 14 March 1983, the House discussed two separate Estimates – for Parliamentary stationery and printing and for development in the Turks and Caicos Islands. No divisions were held. According to Members interested in the experiment, including the chairman of the Select Committee on Procedure (Supply), Terence Higgins, the two half-day debates constituted a useful beginning on which to build. Attendance, though, was low, as it has been in subsequent debates.

Public Accounts Commission

The National Audit Act, introduced as a Private Member's Bill by Norman St John-Stevas, was passed in 1983 despite initial government opposition. The Act recognized the Comptroller and Auditor-General as an officer of the House of Commons and established a National Audit Office (under the Comptroller and Auditor-General) with power to carry out efficiency audits of government departments and certain public bodies.

The office is responsible to a Public Accounts Commission, also established under the terms of the Act. The commission came into being on 1 January 1984 and has a membership of nine Members of Parliament, appointed on 22 December 1983. They are:

Sir Edward du Cann (Con.), chairman
Roy Beggs (Official Ulster Unionist)
John Biffen (Con.), Leader of the House
Sir William Clark (Con.)
William Hamilton (Lab.)
Terence Higgins (Con.)
Sir Peter Hordern (Con.)
Robert Sheldon (Lab.), chairman of the Public Accounts
  Committee
David Young (Lab.)

The Leader of the House of Commons and the chairman of the Public Accounts Committee serve as members *ex officio*. Sir Edward du Cann is a former chairman of the Public Accounts Committee and of the Treasury and Civil Service Select Committee. Indeed, in terms of knowledge of financial procedures, the commission enjoys a heavyweight membership.[6]

Being created under the National Audit Act, the commission is a statutory body and not (like the Public Accounts Committee, with which it is now often confused) a parliamentary committee.

House of Commons Commission

Under the terms of the House of Commons (Administration) Act of 1978, there now exists a House of Commons Commission. It has responsibility for the internal affairs of the House, including staffing, expenditure, pensions and remuneration. Its membership comprises the Speaker (who chairs it), the Leader of the House, one MP nominated by the Leader of the Opposition (usually the Shadow Leader of the House), and three non-ministerialist MPs (including, in practice, a representative of the minority parties – currently Liberal Alan Beith, now the longest-serving member of the commission). The members serving in November 1984 were:

Mr Speaker, chairman
Alan Beith (Lib.)
John Biffen (Con.), Leader of the House
Betty Boothroyd (Lab.)
Sir Paul Bryan (Con.)
Peter Shore (Lab.)

Each year, the commission lays before the House an estimate of the expenses for each of the House's six departments. Like the Public Accounts Commission, it is a statutory body.

The commission is independent of government and the Treasury. Among other things, it approves the funds requested by the Liaison Committee for staffing, travel and other expenses of the select committees. In 1981, the items controlled by the commission amounted to some £14.2 million, a little under a third of the total expenditure on the House. Given this, a number of observers consider that the commission has great scope to shape the internal developments of the House.[7] 'It is', as Geoffrey Lock observed 'a major step forward that the Commons should be, at least in part, masters in their own House financially'.[8]

The commission is accountable to the House through one of its members, who serves as spokesman for it. Parliamentary Questions can be, and are, tabled for answer by this spokesman.

Opposition Days

In 1982, the 29 Supply Days were abolished. These were days on which it was recognized that certain topics, such as Scottish affairs, should be debated and the remainder of topics for discussion chosen by the Opposition. They had little to do with supply. In order to rationalize procedure, they were replaced by 19 Opposition Days, days on which the Opposition was recognized formally as having the right to choose the topics for debate. The subjects regularly dealt with on Supply Days, such as Scottish affairs, the armed services and the EEC, were transferred to be debated in government time.

Other procedural changes

A number of other procedural changes have been approved by the House. These have included a change in the time of sittings on Fridays: the House meets now at 9.30 a.m, instead of 11.00 a.m., and rises at 3.00 p.m. Other changes have covered the rules governing divisions on amendments, provision for Private Members' Bills to be referred to Second Reading Committees (subject to no Member objecting), a limit on the length of debate on Recess Adjournment motions, and changes in the procedure for debate on Consolidated Fund Bills. These and other changes are detailed in the *Factsheets*, numbers 3, 9 and 18, available from the Public Information Office, House of Commons, London SW1A 0AA.

Notes

1 *HL Deb.* 385, col. 254.
2 For example, in 1979 – after the House had voted to retain the existing method of raising points of order during divisions – the Speaker announced that two hats would henceforth be available for use and ruled that substitute headgear, such as Order Papers, would not be acceptable.
3 All-Party House of Commons Reform Group, *Findings of the Survey of MPs' Attitudes to Reform and the Role of the MP* (London: mimeo, 1984), p. 6.
4 B. George MP and B. Evans, 'Parliamentary Reform: The Internal View', in D. Judge (ed.), *The Politics of Parliamentary Reform* (London: Heinemann, 1983), p. 89.
5 H. J. Benyon, 'The House of Commons' Experiment with Special Standing Committees', *Public Law*, Summer 1982, pp. 194–5.
6 The commission includes, in addition to Sir Edward du Cann (the most experienced committee chairman in the House), two former Treasury ministers, Robert Sheldon (now chairman of the Public Accounts Committee) and Terence Higgins (now chairman of the Treasury and Civil Service Select Committee), and two Members who have served as chairmen of the Conservative backbench Finance Committee, Sir Peter Hordern and Sir William Clark.
7 See George and Evans, 'Parliamentary Reform', pp. 93–4.
8 G. Lock, 'The Administrative and Statutory Framework', in M. Rush (ed.), *The House of Commons: Services and Facilities, 1972–1982* (London: Policy Studies Institute, 1983), p. 13.

Appendix 2
Finance and Facilities for MPs

Ken Batty and Bruce George MP

Finance

Pay

Since 1971, MPs' pay and allowances have been reviewed by the Top Salaries Review Body, though the final decision continues to rest with Parliament. The twentieth and most recent report of the committee was presented to Parliament in May 1983.[1] It recommended that 'as at 13th June 1983 a salary of £19,000 is appropriate for Members of Parliament,'[2] though noting that 'well over half of those [MPs] responding to our questionnaire suggested a salary in excess of £20,000 would be appropriate.'[3]

The government, calling for pay restraint from the rest of the nation, clearly felt such a rise was too high (£19,000 per annum would have constituted an increase of about 30 per cent). It suggested instead a rise of 4 per cent, bringing pay to £15,090. Members on both sides of the House objected and a compromise was eventually reached: there was to be an immediate rise of 5.5 per cent – bringing the salary to £15,308 – with annual rises over a five-year period to bring it up to £18,500, after which rises would be as for a senior civil servant earning the same amount.[4]

However, the issue of MPs' pay is still not really resolved. The findings of the Review Body would suggest that the great majority of Members are not satisfied with what they currently receive. The problem is a long-standing one, its roots lying in the evolution of the present House. In the days of the amateur MP, when most Members would have a well-paid career or leisured interest outside the House, the issue of pay was not important. In the twentieth century, and most especially since the Second World War, there has been a change in the nature of the House with more Members becoming 'full time'. Sadly, the House has not adapted to this change. If the old allowances system was to be converted to a proper salary there would need to be a massive increase. Neither the government of the day nor the House has been prepared to take such a step. Attempts to achieve a significant increase in salaries have aroused opposition from government (arguing for pay restraint) and a significant number of Members (seeing service as a public, non-professional duty). The issue has tended to be an emotive one. Government backbenchers were as divided on the issue in 1954 as they were to be in 1979 and 1983.[5]

The intention to link Members' salary with that of civil servants has not solved the problem. Parliament remains sovereign on the issue of pay. What it has done has been to devise a way of keeping the issue out of the public gaze. Yet by doing this it has failed to take the responsibility as it should. If it is true that the modern Member can only function properly with a better salary then let the House say so and act upon that, and thus fulfil to the best of its ability the task for which it was elected.

Table A2.1 shows how MPs' salary has altered over the years and how the current settlement will affect pay up to 1987.

Table A2.1   Salary of Members of Parliament

Year	Salary (£)
Aug. 1911	400
Oct. 1931	360
May 1954	1,250
Oct. 1964	3,250
Jan. 1972	4,500
Jun. 1980	11,750
Jun. 1983	15,308
Jun. 1984	16,106
Jun. 1985	16,904
Jun. 1986	17,702
Jun. 1987	18,500

Source: House of Commons *Factsheet No. 17* (London: House of Commons Public Information Office, 1983).

Allowances

In addition to their salary, MPs receive various allowances to cover a range of possible expenditure. Probably the most important is the 'office equipment, secretarial and research assistance allowance'. Prior to July 1984 the allowance had been adjusted on an *ad hoc* basis, according to what seemed appropriate at the time. However, it was agreed, on the recommendation of the Review Body and with government approval, that 'in future the secretarial, research and office expenses allowance should be increased by the same percentage as the salary, plus London weighting, of a civil servant at the maximum point of the senior personal secretary scale.'[6] If the government's offer to civil servants is accepted then this will be £12,347 per annum – an increase of about 40 per cent. Members also receive help to meet the cost of their secretaries' pensions and extra money should a temporary secretary be required because of illness.

Other allowances include free telephone calls from the Palace of Westminster and free postage, though both with the caveat 'on parliamentary business' and 'internal to the UK'. A travel allowance is given: for cars based on the RAC's figures of mileage costs with a bonus for vehicle depreciation;[7] otherwise, Members receive vouchers for free first-class travel by rail, sea or air between London and the constituency and London and home.[8] There is also a subsistence allowance based on the number of days Parliament sits and from 1974 all MPs representing constituencies in the Greater London area have been eligible for a London allowance.[9]

The thinking behind these allowances is that the Member should not be out of pocket for doing his or her job properly. Clearly, this affects the nature of our democracy, for if it is only the wealthy who can adequately represent their constituents then the wealthy will enjoy disproportionate access to the governing elite. It is clear that many MPs believe that neither the pay nor the allowances are large enough to allow them to fulfil their role to the level one might expect. If that is true, and Members are not thinking merely of themselves, then we have a problem which strikes at the idea of a representative Parliament.

Facilities

Having looked at the pay and allowances Members receive we now turn to the facilities available to them. In doing so, we are limiting the study to what is available to a Member as a Member and not taking into account what he or she may receive as a member of a particular party.[10]

Library

The most obvious facility is the House of Commons Library, which exists to satisfy the research and information demands made upon it by Members of Parliament in pursuit of their parliamentary duties.

In 1932, H. G. Wells said of it:

no effort is made, even from such pathetically inadequate material as this library comprises, to assemble for the use of members from time to time such books or papers as bear on subjects under discussion.... There are no research workers, preparing synopses or abstracts of information, no effort, indeed, at all to relate the library, as·such, to the specific needs of those who might use it.[11]

Since that time there has been a considerable number of changes to make the library a significant source of reference and information. Around 150,000 books and pamphlets are now held in it[12] and it receives over 100 newspapers and about 1,400 journals and periodicals.[13] The library employs a staff of about 100 and is organized into two divisions, the parliamentary division, which is the reference arm, and the research division. The research division alone gives written replies to over 6,000 enquiries each year from Members;[14] the parliamentary division 'handles reference enquiries and book borrowing and provides the Library with its technical services.... requests for information number about 50,000 in the course of a year.'[15]

The library staff are assisted in answering this deluge of requests by POLIS – the Parliamentary On Line Information Service. POLIS was the outcome of various projects using computers to assist in the library which took place in the late 1960s and the 1970s.[16] POLIS is essentially a computerized classification index, but one which allows for a high degree of cross-referencing. Information can be retrieved by subject, Member's name, minister's name, government department, Commitee, Bill or Act. All references are displayed in reverse chronological order which further aids access to the latest information.[17] The library's commitment to the system, and to efficiency in general, is shown in this quotation from one of the POLIS team: 'Our aim is to index and enter items on the day that they appear in the Unit and to have them available for on-line retrieval within twenty-four hours.'[18] A high aim, if not always achieved.

Personal secretary

The House of Commons Library is the only formal non-governmental source of information and assistance specially available to MPs outside party research sources. Consequently, as we have seen, Members receive an allowance to provide for a secretary and a part-time research assistant. That MPs prefer an allowance system to one under which their aides would be employees of the House itself is unquestionable. Phillip Whitehead, who chaired a committee looking at the provision of secretaries and research assistants, commented on the number of MPs 'who have stopped me in the corridors of this place and have asked jocularly "Have you managed to create the typing pool yet?"'[19] A sub-committee of the House of Commons (Services) Committee reported that it had 'received little evidence (and none from Members) in favour of the House itself becoming the employer'.[20] The allowance system is popular in principle, particularly so because what the MP spends it on is his or her own business.

Table A2.2 shows how much in 1981 MPs who responded to the Review Body's questionnaire spent on areas covered by the allowance. It should be noted that the allowance at that time was £8,480.[21]

Research assistance

Whilst the need for a secretary is accepted by most Members, if only to relieve the Member of some of the burden of correspondence, the need for a research assistant is less apparent.

One vital consideration is the Member's own priorities. Given unlimited time, a typical Member might sit in the chamber all the time that the House sits, having first read around the topics under discussion. He or she might also specialize in great depth in one or more sectors of public policy. He might also sit on a select committee and on occasion a standing committee, having first studied the subject deeply. He might also crusade on behalf of constituents and play a leading role in a national pressure group. Indeed, he might do a million-and-one things if his time were unlimited. Of course, it is not, so Members have to have an agenda of priorities. For no two Members are these likely to be the same. Consequently, one Member might find that he has no requirement for a research assistant, while another might feel that to fulfil his priorities he must have help in the routine task of ferreting out information and in the more specialized task of organizing that information into a logical and concise framework. That the library will assist in this task is true; however, it is increasingly

Table A2.2 MPs: distribution of secretarial and other office expenditure

		Nil	1–99	100–249	250–499	500–999	1,000–1,999	2,000–3,999	4,000–4,999	5,000–5,999	6,000–6,999	7,000–7,999	8,000–8,999	9,000–9,999	10,000–10,999	11,000–12,999	13,000 and over	Total giving details	Mean expenditure[a]
Secretarial assistance[b]	No.	–	–	–	–	–	3	18	18	33	61	82	36	7	2	2	3	265	6,800
	%	–	–	–	–	–	1	7	7	12	23	31	14	3	1	1	1	100	
Research assistance	No.	182	1	3	7	16	43	32	10	4	5	1	1	1	–	–	–	306	950
	%	59	0	1	2	5	14	10	3	1	2	0	0	0	–	–	–	100	
Travel expenses of staff	No.	162	29	44	19	18	6	1	–	1	–	–	–	–	–	–	–	280	150
	%	58	10	16	7	7	2	0	–	0	–	–	–	–	–	–	–	100	
Purchase of office equipment[c]	No.	64	15	62	49	49	16	2	1	–	–	–	–	–	–	–	–	258	400
	%	25	6	24	19	19	6	1	0	–	–	–	–	–	–	–	–	100	
Maintenance of office equipment	No.	64	84	78	15	8	3	1	–	–	–	–	–	–	–	–	–	253	150
	%	25	33	31	6	3	1	0	–	–	–	–	–	–	–	–	–	100	
Other office expenses[d]	No.	51	27	39	43	55	32	20	–	–	–	1	–	–	–	–	–	268	650
	%	19	10	15	16	21	12	7	–	–	–	0	–	–	–	–	–	100	
Total expenditure	No.	–	–	–	–	–	–	7	4	7	20	56	71	33	21	22	14	255	8,800
	%	–	–	–	–	–	–	3	2	3	8	22	28	13	8	9	5	100	

Expenditure in the range (£)

The figures have not been adjusted to accommodate the different years for which Members gave information.

In most cases the figures related to either year beginning April 1981 or the year beginning October 1981.

[a] Means include those with zero expenditure. Components do not add up to the total, mainly because different numbers of replies have been used.

[b] Includes the use of agency staff; excludes Members' national insurance contributions as employers.

[c] Includes leasing.

[d] Includes, for example, expenses of constituency office or surgeries and postage and telephone costs. Also includes expenditure on other items, such as office equipment, for which separate details were not provided.

Source: Review Body on Top Salaries, Review of Parliamentary Pay and Allowances, twentieth report, Cmnd 8881 (London: HMSO, 1983) vol. II, table 23, p. 33.

hard-pressed to deal with its workload and cannot always give Members the attention either the staff or the Members would wish. Furthermore, by the nature of his role, the MP is interested in having information presented in a particular way and 'the work of research assistants [has] a political dimension which Library staff would not wish to provide.'[22]

As a result, research assistants are becoming increasingly common around the House. The responses to the questionnaire administered by the Commons' Reform Group in 1984 suggest that a little over 50 per cent of Members employ a researcher on a full- or part-time basis.[23] The spread of assistants, though, is not uniform across the House, either across the parties or across the length of time a Member has served. As tables A2.3 and A2.4 show, newer MPs are more likely to have researchers than their longer-serving colleagues, and a Conservative Member is less likely to have one than a Labour Member and a Labour Member is less likely to have one than an Alliance Member. The main reason for this, we would suggest, is a difference in the perception of the Member's role. Longer-serving Members hark back to a time when it was customary for a Member to have a career outside the House – which, rather paradoxically, made them less likely to seek help when they were in the House. Even now Conservative Members are more likely than others to have outside occupations. Furthermore, their attitude to the job is somewhat different. The percentage of Alliance Members with research assistants, however, has more to do with the absence of a party-based research service than a difference in priorities.

Table A2.3   MPs employing research assistants: by party, 1984

Party	Full-time (%)	Part-time (%)	None (%)
Conservative	3.8	46.2	50.0
Labour	10.8	48.2	40.9
Alliance	29.4	52.9	17.6
Other	12.5	62.5	25.0
Total	7.2	47.5	45.3

Response rate to questionnaire: 49.8 per cent.
Source: All-Party House of Commons Reform Group, *Findings of the Survey of MPs' Attitudes to Reform and the Role of the MP* (London: mimeo, 1984), p. 23.

Table A2.4   Division of research assistants according to date employing Member elected

	MPs employing research assistants in 1982–3[a]
Date elected	(%)
1945–50	1.9
1950–60	7.2
1960–70	23.1
1970–80	66.8
1980–2	1.0
	100.0

[a]Calculated by number with permits.

Source: M. Keegan, 'Research Assistants in the House of Commons', unpublished undergraduate dissertation, University of Exeter Politics Department.

Given that different Members have different attitudes to what the job entails, it follows that the tasks they give their secretaries and research assistants will differ. Furthermore, a task that one Member gives to his researcher another may give to his secretary. Indeed, this overlap was shown when the Review Body found in carrying out its survey that the division between secretary and researcher was so blurred that 36 per cent of respondents saw their job as a combination of the two.[24] Tables A2.5 and A2.6 show how all the respondents to the survey – secretaries, researchers or those who described themselves as a combination of the two – divided their day. It is interesting to note that one of the largest consumers of time for both secretaries and secretaries/research assistants is answering letters on behalf of the Member. Clearly, much of the Member's time would be spent doing this if he did not have assistance. Moreover, although (as shown in chapter 4) grievance-chasing for constituents is clearly an important function for MPs, it often does not require their personal attention to chase up casework: they could be doing something else and thus, in conjunction with their team, be more efficient.

Conclusion

The whole issue of finance and facilities for MPs has a basic question at its root: What do we see as the role of our MPs? If we expect a

Table A2.5 MPs' secretaries and secretaries/research assistants: distribution of working time

Activity	Secretaries		Secretaries/ research assistants	
			When House is:	
	Sitting (%)	In recess (%)	Sitting (%)	In recess (%)
Typing				
Shorthand	32	28	18	15
Audio	8	8	5	5
Word-processing	1	1	0	0
Copy-typing	3	3	2	2
Total	43	40	25	22
Secretarial				
Appointments etc., e.g. keeping diary, making travel arrangements, looking after visitors, dealing with constituents	15	12	13	12
Correspondence and filing, e.g. opening and acknowledging letters, filing documents, photocopying, assembling papers for meetings	16	16	14	14
Answering letters, i.e. drafting replies or replying on behalf of Member	20	25	33	37
Telephone calls not covered above	5	5	6	7
Total	55	58	66	68

Table A2.5 continued

| | Secretaries | | Secretaries/ research assistants | |
| | When House is: | | | |
Activity	Sitting (%)	In recess (%)	Sitting (%)	In recess (%)
Other				
Research and writing reports	0	0	5	6
Work on constituency matters	0	0	2	2
Dealing with press releases, press cuttings, etc.	–	1	1	1
Chauffeuring, errands, etc., for Member	1	1	1	1
Other	0	1	1	1
Total	2	2	9	9
	100	100	100	100
Total				
(Mean hours worked per week)	36.2	31.3	39.3	32.9)
(Number of replies used)	115	115	84	84

Source: Review Body on Top Salaries, Review of Parliamentary Pay and Allowances, twentieth report, Cmnd 8881 (London: HMSO, 1983), vol. II, table 2, p. 49.

Table A2.6   MPs' research assistants: distribution of working time

| | When House is: | |
| | Sitting | In recess |
Activity	(%)	(%)
Research, writing papers, speeches, press releases and summaries, briefing Member	58	57
Constituency matters, research and action	14	14
Reading newspapers, journals, Bills, etc.	9	7
Clerical work, e.g. typing, filing, photocopying	8	8
Dealing with correspondence	4	5
Meetings with e.g. constituents, pressure groups	4	4
Other	2	5
Total	100	100
(Mean hours worked per week	30.0	24.8)
(Number of replies used	26	26)

Source: Review Body on Top Salaries, *Review of Parliamentary Pay and Allowances*, twentieth report, Cmnd 8881 vol. II, table 2, p. 49.

half-hearted commitment from a part-timer who has failed in his chosen career then let us say so – and reward accordingly. However, we would suggest this is far from the public expectation. The public, we think, would like to see the very top men and women from society, those with ability and commitment, to represent them. Yet the pay and the facilities of the House are such that when such people do stand it is not because of the attractions of pay and rewards commensurate with the task – they are not there. The pay of British MPs is no better than that of middle management in industry or commerce. Their facilities in terms of office space and back-up staff do not even match middle-management levels. The House still seems to support the ethos of the amateur Member. We are asking our representatives to meet the challenges of the 1980s with resources that show an attitude based in the 1930s. It is notable that the Clerks of the House receive more than Members,[25] a disparity that reflects the continuation of the perception of Members as the amateurs in the parliamentary process.

Ideally, the House should attract the very top people and they should be rewarded accordingly. Furthermore, they should receive support and back-up to enable them to carry out their role adequately. The continuing failure of the House to match public expectation is substantially due to the inadequate resources at its disposal. If this situation continues, and is matched by a continuing trend of bureaucratization and increasing government involvement, then we will soon reach the point where the House can no longer provide an effective check on government. We are not suggesting that more and better facilities are a panacea for Britain's political malaise but we would suggest that without them we cannot expect our representatives to begin to conquer it.

Notes

1 Review Body on Top Salaries, *Review of Parliamentary Pay and Allowances*, twentieth report, Cmnd 8881 (London: HMSO, 1983).
2 Ibid., para. 23.
3 Ibid., para. 24.
4 House of Commons *Factsheet No. 17* (London: House of Commons Public Information Office, 1983).
5 See, e.g., *HC Deb.* 528, cols 149–58 (1954), and P. Norton, *The Commons in Perspective* (Oxford: Martin Robertson, 1981), p. 119.
6 John Biffen, Leader of the House, 20 July 1984: *HC Deb.* 64, col. 619.
7 Ibid.
8 *Review Body*, vol. II, table 3, p. 118.
9 M. Rush (ed.), *The House of Commons: Services and Facilities, 1972–1982* (London: Policy Studies Institute, 1983).
10 In a party capacity, Members enjoy the research resources (in so far as they exist) of their party headquarters; this is especially so on the Conservative side of the House, where the resources of Conservative Research Department are available. In addition, the parliamentary parties receive public funds – the so-called Short Money – to help them fulfil their parliamentary duties. The amount provided is £1,080 for each seat won by the party concerned plus £2.16 for every 200 votes cast for it at the preceding general election, providing that the maximum payable shall not exceed £325,000. *HC Deb.* 38, col. 810–11.
11 H. G. Wells, 'The Work, Wealth and Happiness of Mankind', quoted in J. B. Poole, G. Scott and C. W. H. Ellis, 'Information Retrieval from Hansard and Statute Law', *Parliamentary Affairs*, 29(4) Autumn 1976, p. 421.
12 D. Menhennet, 'Library Research Service', *The House Magazine*, 4 February 1983, p. 4.
13 J. B. Poole, 'The Work of the House of Commons Library', *The Information Scientist*, March 1974, p. 13.
14 D. Menhennet, 'Library Research Service', *The House Magazine*, 10 December 1982, p. 4.

15 P. Laundy, *Parliamentary Librarianship in the English-Speaking World* (London: Library Association, 1980) pp. 31 and 33.
16 See, for instance, J. B. Poole, 'Information Services for the Commons: A Computer Experiment', *Parliamentary Affairs*, Spring 1969 – on the Culham project. Also J. B. Poole and J. A. van Dongen, 'A Computerised Macro-Economic Data Service for Parliament: The MEDHOC Project', *Program*, January 1975.
17 D. Englefield, 'Copperplate to Computer', *The House Magazine*, 26 November 1982.
18 R. Wheatman, 'POLIS at Westminster', *Law Librarian*, December 1981, p. 58.
19 Speaking in the Commons, 21 February 1978: *HC Deb.* 944, col. 1358.
20 *Second Report from the House of Commons (Services) Committee, Session 1976/77* (London: HMSO, 1977), para. 9.
21 *Factsheet No. 17*, p. 7.
22 D. Englefield, *Parliament and Information* (London: Longman, 1981), p. 53.
23 M. Keegan, 'Research Assistance in the House of Commons', unpublished undergraduate dissertation, University of Exeter Politics Department, p. 18.
24 *Review & Parliamentary Pay and Allowances*, p. 48.
25 A Senior Clerk receives a minimum of £13,649 per annum; the Clerk of the House receives £42,750 (1984 figures).

Contributors

Dr Nicholas Baldwin is Lecturer in Politics and Government at Wroxton College of Fairleigh Dickinson University. He graduated in Politics from the University of Hull in 1979 and in 1985 received his PhD from Exeter University for his thesis on the House of Lords. He has published articles on the powers and composition of the Upper House.

Ken Batty is a business executive. He graduated in Politics from the University of Hull in 1983. He is currently undertaking research (with Bruce George) on comparative pay and facilities in legislatures.

Stephen Downs is Assistant Secretary of Leeds Chamber of Commerce. He graduated in Politics from the University of Hull in 1979, subsequently undertaking research on the role of the Select Committee on Education, Science and Arts.

Bruce George is Labour Member of Parliament for Walsall South. He was previously a lecturer in Politics. Elected in 1974, he has served on the Select Committee on Defence since it was created in 1979. He is the author of a number of articles on select committees and parliamentary reform.

Cliff Grantham is a journalist working for BBC local radio. He graduated with a First in Politics and Sociology from the University of Hull in 1984.

James Marsh is a committee clerk with the London Borough of Lambeth. He graduated in Politics from the University of Hull in

1979, subsequently undertaking postgraduate research on MP–constituency relationships.

Caroline Moore Hodgson is a business executive. She graduated in Politics and Sociology from the University of Hull in 1979. As an undergraduate, she completed research on the European Communities Committee of the House of Lords.

Dr Philip Norton is Reader in Politics at the University of Hull. He is the author of *The British Polity* (London: Longman, 1984), *The Constitution in Flux* (Oxford: Basil Blackwell, 1982), *The Commons in Perspective* (Oxford: Martin Robertson, 1981), *Conservatives and Conservatism*, with A. Aughey (London: Temple Smith, 1981), *Dissension in the House of Commons 1974–1979* (Oxford: Oxford University Press, 1980), *Conservative Dissidents* (London: Temple Smith, 1978), *Dissension in the House of Commons 1945–74* (London: Macmillan, 1975), editor of *Law and Order and British Politics* (Farnborough: Gower, 1984), and has contributed numerous articles to learned journals and other works on Parliament. He is a member of the executive committees of the Political Studies Association of the United Kingdom, the Study of Parliament Group (serving as its academic secretary 1981–85), and the British Politics Group in the USA, and a member of the Committee of Co-operation for European Parliamentary Studies.

Select Reading List

This work seeks to supplement existing texts by providing an analysis of recent developments in both Houses of Parliament. It also covers a number of topics previously neglected in texts on Parliament. As such, reliance on existing published sources is limited. What follows, therefore, is not a bibliography but a short guide to existing texts, texts which are supplemented by the preceding chapters.

The House of Commons

General and comparative works

For a general introduction to the structures, procedures and behaviour of the House of Commons, the most comprehensive text is P. Norton, *The Commons in Perspective* (Oxford: Martin Robertson, 1981). Also widely used but less comprehensive is S. A. Walkland and M. Ryle (eds), *The Commons Today* (London: Fontana, 1981). The best work on comparative legislatures is M. Mezey, *Comparative Legislatures* (Durham, NC: Duke University Press, 1979). A recent article concentrating on the Commons in comparative perspective is P. Norton, 'Parliament and Policy in Britain: The House of Commons as a Policy Influencer', *Teaching Politics*, 13(2), May 1984, pp. 198–221.

Behavioural changes

On changes in voting behaviour in the Commons, the most important works are by the editor of this volume: P. Norton, *Dissension in the House of Commons 1974–1979* (Oxford: Oxford University Press, 1980), *Conservative Dissidents* (London: Temple Smith, 1978) and *Dissension in the House of Commons 1945–74* (London: Macmillan, 1975). On government defeats in standing committees, see J. E. Schwarz, 'Exploring a New Role in Policy-making: The British House of Commons in the 1970s', *American Political Science Review*,

74(1), March 1980, pp. 23–37. On the constitutional implications of defeats in the division lobbies, see P. Norton, 'Government Defeats in the House of Commons: Myth and Reality', *Public Law*, Winter 1978, pp. 360–78. More generally, see S. H. Beer, *Britain Against Itself* (London: Faber & Faber, 1982), pp. 180–94, and L. D. Epstein, 'What Happened to the British Party Model?', *American Political Science Review*, 74(1), March 1980, pp. 9–22.

Structural changes

A major new study of the new select committees, by members of the Study of Parliament Group, is to be published in the summer of 1985 by Oxford University Press. Already published works include D. Englefield (ed.), *Commons Select Committees: Catalysts for Progress?* (London: Longman, 1984), which includes much useful data on the committee in the 1979–83 Parliament. Also valuable are the reports from the chairmen of the committees, published in *The First Report from the Liaison Committee*, HC 92 (London: HMSO, 1982). Other published assessments include A. Davies, *Reformed Select Committees: The First Year* (London: Outer Circle Policy Unit, 1980), B. George and B. Evans, 'Parliamentary Reform: The Internal View', in D. Judge (ed.), *The Politics of Parliamentary Reform* (London: Heinemann, 1983), pp. 70–95; and D. Hill (ed.), *Parliamentary Select Committees in Action: A Symposium*, Strathclyde Papers on Government and Politics (Glasgow: Strathclyde University Politics Department, 1984). On the development of select committees, see N. Johnson, 'Select Committees and Administration', in S. A. Walkland (ed.), *The House of Commons in the Twentieth Century* (Oxford: Oxford University Press, 1979), pp. 426–75.

Representational changes

There have been few systematic studies of an MP's constituency role. Some Members refer to it in their memoirs. Otherwise the only published material is in article or chapter form. Foremost among this are the articles by B. Cain, J. Ferejohn and M. Fiorina: 'The House is Not a Home: British MPs in their Constituencies', *Legislative Studies Quarterly*, 4(4), November 1979, pp. 501–23, and 'The Constituency Service Basis of the Personal Vote for U.S. Representatives and British Members of Parliament', *American Political Science Review*, 78(1), March 1984, pp. 110–25. See also B. Cain, 'Blessed be the Ties that Unbind: Constituency Work and the Vote Swing in Great Britain', *Political Studies*, 31(1), March 1983, pp. 103–11, and B. Cain and D. B. Ritchie, 'Constituency Involvement: Hemel Hempstead', *Parliamentary Affairs*, 35(1), Winter 1982, pp. 73–83.

Other articles worthy of consultation are R. Dinnage, 'Parliamentary Advice Bureau', *New Society*, 24 February 1972; A. Beith MP, 'The MP as a Grievance Chaser', *Public Administration Bulletin*, August 1976, pp. 6–10; R. Munroe, 'The Member of Parliament as Representative: The View from the Constituency', *Political Studies*, 25(4), December 1977, pp. 577–87; I. Crewe,

'Electoral Reform and the Local MP', in S. E. Finer (ed.), *Adversary Politics and Electoral Reform* (London: Wigram, 1975), pp. 317–42; P. Norton, '"Dear Minister . . ." The importance of MP-to-Minister Correspondence', *Parliamentary Affairs*, 35(1), Winter 1982, pp. 59–72; and the pamphlet by F. Morrell, *From the Electors of Bristol* (Nottingham: Spokesman Books, 1977).

The House of Lords

There is no one good up-to-date text devoted to the House of Lords. P. Bromhead, *The House of Lords and Contemporary Politics 1911–1957* (London: Routledge & Kegan Paul, 1958) is now much too dated. J. Morgan, *The House of Lords and the Labour Government 1964–70* (Oxford: Oxford University Press, 1975) provides an interesting case study. For recent articles, see especially D. Shell, 'The House of Lords', in D. Judge (ed.), *The Politics of Parliamentary Reform* (London: Heinemann, 1983), pp. 96–113, and N. Baldwin, 'The House of Lords: Its Constitution and Functions', *Exeter Research Group: Discussion Paper 9* (Exeter: Exeter University, 1982). Texts and pamphlets on reform of the Upper House are cited below.

On structural changes, no major study exists of the Lords' use of committees. However, a summary of the work of the European Communities Committee appears in F. E. C. Gregory, *Dilemmas of Government* (Oxford: Martin Robertson, 1983), pp. 113–20, and the forthcoming study on select committees, by members of the Study of Parliament Group (referred to above), will include a chapter on Lords' committees by T. St John Bates. See also D. Brew, 'National Parliamentary Scrutiny of European Community Legislation', in V. Herman and R. van Schendelen (eds), *The European Parliament and National Parliaments* (Farnborough: Saxon House, 1979). Also worthy of research are the reports issued by the European Communities Committee and other Lords' committees.

Conclusion

On the various proposals for reform of the House of Commons, see especially P. Norton, *The Commons in Perspective* (Oxford: Martin Robertson, 1981); S. E. Finer (ed.), *Adversary Politics and Electoral Reform* (London: Wigram, 1975); *The First Report from the Select Committee on Procedure, Session 1977/78*, HC 588 (London: HMSO, 1978); D. Judge (ed.), *The Politics of Parliamentary Reform* (London: Heinemann, 1983); and P. Norton, *The Constitution in Flux* (Oxford: Martin Robertson, 1982; Basil Blackwell, 1984). The latter work covers the major constitutional reform proposals.

On reform of the House of Lords, see *The First Report from the House of Lords' Select Committee on Practice and Procedure*, HL 141 (London: HMSO, 1977); P. Norton, *The Constitution in Flux*, ch. 6; J. Morgan, 'The House of Lords in the 1980s', *The Parliamentarian*, 62(1), January 1981, pp. 18–26; *The*

House of Lords: Report of the Conservative Review Committee (London: Conservative Central Office, 1978); Lord Chalfont, 'Reform of the House of Lords', *The Parliamentarian*, 58(4), October 1977, pp. 233–9; Lord Boyd-Carpenter, 'Reform of the House of Lords: Another View', *The Parliamentarian*, 59(2), April 1978, pp. 90–3; and S. Bell, *How to Abolish the Lords*, Fabian Tract 476 (London: Fabian Society, 1981). More generally, see the Report of a Study Group of the Commonwealth Parliamentary Association, 'The Role of Second Chambers', *The Parliamentarian*, 63(4), October 1982.

On proposals for comprehensive constitutional change, see N. Johnson, *In Search of the Constitution* (London: Methuen, 1980); the Liberal Party Reform of Government Panel, *A New Constitutional Settlement* (London: Liberal Publications Department, 1980); and P. Norton, *The Constitution in Flux*, Conclusions.

Index

Schwarz, J., 23, 28, 41
Science and Technology, Select
  Committee on: Commons, 15,
  56, 117, 140; Lords, 16, 115–17,
  154
Scotland, 9, 146, 147, 150, 167
Scotland and Wales Bill, 26, 41,
  147
Scotland Bill, 26–7
select committees: Commons, 15,
  41–2, 44, 48–67, 114–15, 117,
  138, 140, 142, 143–4, 155,
  163–4, 167; Lords, 115–32, 153,
  154; *see also* under the names of
  individual committees (e.g.
  Agriculture, Select Committee
  on)
Selection, Select Committee of:
  Commons, 61; Lords, 120
Sexual Discrimination, Select
  Committee on (Lords), 115
Sheldon, R., 166
Shell, D., 130
Shore, P., 166
Small Charities, Select Committee
  on (Lords), 115
Smith, T. A., 80
Social Democratic Party (SDP), 10,
  109; *see also* Alliance, SDP/
  Liberal
Social Security, 76
Social Services, 73
Social Services, Secretary of State
  for, 33
Speaker, Mr, 32, 36, 166
Spearing, N., 126
special standing committees, 67,
  142, 158–9, 164–5
standing committees: Commons,
  15, 27–8, 50, 51, 55–6, 67, 124,
  141, 142, 164; Lords, 114
Statutory Instruments, Joint
  Committee on, 114
Stoke-on-Trent, 82
Strauss, G., 86

Study of Parliament Group (SPG),
  141, 158
Supply Days, 141, 167

Telecommunications Bill, 101
televising parliament: Commons,
  142; Select Committees, 142
Thatcher, Mrs M., 9, 31, 35–6, 39,
  41, 42
Top Salaries, Review Body on, 169,
  171, 173, 176
Trade and industry, Department of,
  126
trade unions, 9, 10
Trades Union Bill, 101
Trades Union Congress (TUC),
  11, 12, 116, 126, 129
transport, fares, 31, 99
Treasury, Financial Secretary to,
  87
Treasury and Civil Service, Select
  Committee on, 53, 62, 166
Turks and Caicos Islands, 165
Tweedsmuir, Baroness, 120, 128

Unemployment, Select Committee
  on (Lords), 16, 116–117
Utrecht, Treaty of, 96

Verba, S., 89, 137

Wade, Lord, 115
Wakeham, J., 33
Wales, 9, 146, 147, 150
Wales Bill, 26–7
Walkland, S. A., 138, 147, 150–1
Weatherill, B., 36
Wedderburn, Lord, 156
Wheare, Sir K., 2
Wheeler, J., 53
Whigs, 96
Whips: Commons, 22, 28, 36, 39,
  40, 41, 61, 67; Lords, 96, 99,
  101, 109
White, Baroness, 120

20   73